AGRICULTURE ISSUES AND POLICIES

THE FARM SAFETY NET

KEY COMPONENTS

AGRICULTURE ISSUES AND POLICIES

Additional books in this series can be found on Nova's website under the Series tab.

Additional e-books in this series can be found on Nova's website under the e-book tab.

AGRICULTURE ISSUES AND POLICIES

THE FARM SAFETY NET

KEY COMPONENTS

JODIE R. HAGGARD
EDITOR

NOVINKA

New York

Library of Congress Cataloging-in-Publication Data

ISBN: 978-1-63463-731-2

Published by Nova Science Publishers, Inc. † New York

CONTENTS

PREFACE

The federal crop insurance program is considered by many farmers and policy makers as the centerpiece of the farm safety net. The program makes available subsidized insurance policies for about 130 commodities ranging from apples to wheat. These "multiple peril" policies help producers manage financial risks associated with crop yield or revenue losses. Insurable causes of losses include adverse weather (e.g., drought and flood), insects or disease outbreaks, and failure of irrigation water supply. The enacted 2014 farm bill enhances the federal crop insurance program by expanding its scope, covering a greater share of farm losses, and making a variety of other modifications that broaden policy coverage. This book describes in detail changes made to the program as part of the 2014 farm bill. It also discusses the agricultural disaster assistance.

Chapter 1 - The enacted 2014 farm bill (the Agricultural Act of 2014; P.L. 113-79) enhances the federal crop insurance program by expanding its scope, covering a greater share of farm losses, and making other modifications that broaden policy coverage. The changes stem from the desire of many in Congress, particularly members of the agriculture committees, to bolster what they consider to be the most significant aspect of the farm safety net.

Under the federal crop insurance program, which is administered by the U.S. Department of Agriculture's Risk Management Agency (RMA), producers purchase subsidized policies to help manage financial risks associated with crop yield or revenue losses, primarily from natural disasters. In contrast, farm commodity programs apply to a narrower set of "program" crops, require no participation fees, and make payments when prices fall below statutory minimums or when crop revenue is low relative to historical levels.

A prominent crop insurance feature of the 2014 farm bill is the authorization of policies designed to reimburse "shallow losses"—an insured producer's out-of-pocket loss associated with the policy deductible. A new crop insurance policy called Stacked Income Protection Plan (STAX) is made available for upland cotton producers, while the Supplemental Coverage Option (SCO) is made available for other crops. The STAX policy indemnifies losses in county revenue of greater than 10% of expected revenue but not more than the deductible level (e.g., 25%) selected by the producer for the underlying individual policy. (It can also be purchased as a stand-alone policy.) Similarly, SCO is based on expected county revenue (or yields) and covers part of the deductible under the producer's underlying policy. The government subsidy as a share of the policy premium is set at 80% for STAX and 65% for SCO.

A variety of additional provisions are expected to expand existing crop insurance products or require examination of the potential for new products, including those that would benefit specialty crops and animal agriculture. Provisions revise the value of crop insurance for organic crops to reflect generally higher prices of organic (not conventional) crops. USDA is also required to conduct more research on whole farm revenue insurance with higher coverage levels than currently available. Studies or policies are also required for insuring (1) specialty crop producers for food safety and contamination-related losses, (2) swine producers for a catastrophic disease event, (3) producers of catfish against reduction in the margin between the market prices and production costs, (4) commercial poultry production against business disruptions caused by integrator bankruptcy, (5) poultry producers for a catastrophic event, (6) producers of biomass sorghum or sweet sorghum grown as feedstock for renewable energy, and (7) alfalfa producers. A peanut revenue insurance product and rice margin insurance also are mandated. Another provision provides funding for index weather insurance for protecting against weather.

To address conservation concerns, the 2014 farm bill links eligibility for crop insurance premium subsidies to compliance with wetland and conservation requirements for highly erodible land. Also, crop insurance subsidies are reduced for plantings on native sod acreage in certain states.

In total, the crop insurance title increases funding for crop insurance by an additional $5.7 billion over 10 years relative to projected levels that assumed no change in policy. The largest cost items are for STAX ($3.3 billion) and SCO ($1.7 billion), according to the Congressional Budget Office. A controversial item not included in P.L. 113-79 was the reduction of premium subsidies for high-income farmers, which had been included in the Senate farm bill but not the House bill.

Chapter 2 - The farm commodity program provisions in Title I of the Agricultural Act of 2014 (P.L. 113-79, the 2014 farm bill) include three types of support for crop years 2014-2018:

- *Price Loss Coverage (PLC) payments,* which are triggered when the national average farm price for a covered commodity (e.g., wheat, corn, soybeans, rice, and peanuts) is below its statutorily fixed "reference price";
- *Agriculture Risk Coverage (ARC) payments,* as an alternative to PLC, which are triggered when crop revenue is below its guaranteed level based on a multiyear moving average of historical crop revenue; and
- *Marketing Assistance Loans (MALs),* which offer interim financing for the loan commodities (covered crops plus several others) and, if prices fall below loan rates set in statute, additional low-price protection, sometimes paid as *loan deficiency payments (LDPs).*

The enacted 2014 farm bill eliminated "direct payments," which were provided annually to producers and landowners of covered commodities from 1996 to 2013 based on historical production and a fixed payment rate set in statute. All farm program support now consists of variable payments. The PLC and ARC programs are enhanced relative to their predecessors via higher reference prices for PLC and more "local" coverage for ARC (whereby payments are triggered by county or individual losses rather than at the state level). In a major departure from previous farm bills and in response to a trade dispute with Brazil, upland cotton is no longer a covered commodity, with support for that crop now provided by a new crop insurance policy called the Stacked Income Protection Plan (STAX).

Approximately three-fourths of the 10-year, $47 billion in savings associated with the elimination of 2008 farm bill commodity programs was used to offset the costs of revising the overall farm safety net, specifically farm programs in Title I of the 2014 farm bill, adding permanent disaster assistance (also in Title I), enhancing the permanently authorized federal crop insurance program (Title XI), and enhancing the Noninsured Crop Disaster Assistance Program or NAP (Title XII). Crop insurance is available for more than 100 crops, including fruits and vegetables, and is designed primarily to cover losses from natural disasters. Farm programs do not require a participation fee, while crop insurance requires participating farmers to pay part of program costs.

The enacted 2014 farm bill sets a $125,000 per person cap on the total of PLC, ARC, marketing loan gains and loan deficiency payments. The limit applies to the total from all covered commodities except peanuts, which has a separate $125,000 limit. Also, to be eligible for payments, persons must be "actively engaged" in farming. The 2014 farm bill instructs USDA to write regulations (beginning with the 2015 crop year) that define "significant contribution of active personal management" to more clearly and objectively implement existing law. A single, total adjusted gross income (AGI) limit for payment eligibility is established at $900,000, which is less than the sum of the two separate limits (farm and non-farm) in the 2008 farm bill.

The Congressional Budget Office cost estimate (score) of the Title I provisions represents five-year savings of $6.3 billion and 10-year savings of $14.3 billion (both relative to baseline projections made in May 2013 assuming continuation of the 2008 farm bill). If these scores are added to the 2013 CBO baseline of budget outlays used to write the farm bill, then CBO's estimated cost of Title I is $23.6 billion for FY2014-2018 and $44.5 billion over 10 years.

Chapter 3 - The U.S. Department of Agriculture (USDA) offers several programs to help farmers recover financially from natural disasters, including drought and floods. All the programs have permanent authorization, and only one requires a federal disaster designation (the emergency loan program). Most programs receive funding amounts that are "such sums as necessary" and are not subject to annual discretionary appropriations.

The federal crop insurance program offers subsidized policies designed to protect crop producers from unavoidable risks associated with adverse weather, and weather-related plant diseases and insect infestations. Policies must be purchased prior to the planting season. Eligible commodities include most major crops and many specialty crops (including fruit, tree nut, vegetable, and nursery crops), as well as forage and pastureland for livestock producers. The enacted 2014 farm bill (the Agricultural Act of 2014; P.L. 113-79) enhances the crop insurance program by expanding its scope, covering a greater share of farm losses, and making other modifications that broaden policy coverage. Producers who grow a crop that is currently ineligible for crop insurance may apply for the Noninsured Crop Disaster Assistance Program (NAP).

The 2014 farm bill also permanently authorizes three disaster programs for livestock and one for fruit trees, making nearly all parts of the U.S. farm sector covered by a standing disaster program. The programs cover losses beginning in FY2012. USDA began signup on April 15, 2014, ahead of other farm bill programs. Producers do not pay a fee to participate. The programs are:

1) the Livestock Indemnity Program (LIP), which provides payments to eligible livestock owners and contract growers at a rate of 75% of market value for livestock deaths in excess of normal mortality caused by adverse weather;
2) the Livestock Forage Disaster Program (LFP), which makes payments to eligible livestock producers who have suffered grazing losses on drought-affected pasture or grazing land, or on rangeland managed by a federal agency due to a qualifying fire;
3) the Emergency Assistance for Livestock, Honey Bees, and Farm-Raised Fish Program (ELAP), which provides payments (capped at $20 million per year) to producers of livestock, honey bees, and farm-raised fish as compensation for losses due to disease, adverse weather, and feed or water shortages; and
4) the Tree Assistance Program (TAP), making payments to orchardists/nursery tree growers for losses in excess of 15% to replant trees, bushes, and vines damaged by natural disasters.

Separately, for all types of farms and ranches, when a county has been declared a disaster area by either the President or the Secretary of Agriculture, producers in that county may become eligible for low-interest emergency disaster (EM) loans.

USDA has several permanent disaster assistance programs that help producers repair damaged land following natural disasters. It also has authority (prohibited in FY2014) to issue disaster payments to farmers with funds from "Section 32" or the Commodity Credit Corporation (CCC). Finally, USDA can use a variety of existing programs to address disaster issues as they arise, such as allowing emergency grazing on land enrolled in the Conservation Reserve Program.

In: The Farm Safety Net: Key Components ISBN: 978-1-63463-731-2
Editor: Jodie R. Haggard

Chapter 1

CROP INSURANCE PROVISIONS IN THE 2014 FARM BILL (P.L. 113-79)*

Dennis A. Shields

SUMMARY

The enacted 2014 farm bill (the Agricultural Act of 2014; P.L. 113-79) enhances the federal crop insurance program by expanding its scope, covering a greater share of farm losses, and making other modifications that broaden policy coverage. The changes stem from the desire of many in Congress, particularly members of the agriculture committees, to bolster what they consider to be the most significant aspect of the farm safety net.

Under the federal crop insurance program, which is administered by the U.S. Department of Agriculture's Risk Management Agency (RMA), producers purchase subsidized policies to help manage financial risks associated with crop yield or revenue losses, primarily from natural disasters. In contrast, farm commodity programs apply to a narrower set of "program" crops, require no participation fees, and make payments when prices fall below statutory minimums or when crop revenue is low relative to historical levels.

A prominent crop insurance feature of the 2014 farm bill is the authorization of policies designed to reimburse "shallow losses"—an

* This is an edited, reformatted and augmented version of a Congressional Research Service publication R43494, prepared for Members and Committees of Congress dated April 22, 2014.

insured producer's out-of-pocket loss associated with the policy deductible. A new crop insurance policy called Stacked Income Protection Plan (STAX) is made available for upland cotton producers, while the Supplemental Coverage Option (SCO) is made available for other crops. The STAX policy indemnifies losses in county revenue of greater than 10% of expected revenue but not more than the deductible level (e.g., 25%) selected by the producer for the underlying individual policy. (It can also be purchased as a stand-alone policy.) Similarly, SCO is based on expected county revenue (or yields) and covers part of the deductible under the producer's underlying policy. The government subsidy as a share of the policy premium is set at 80% for STAX and 65% for SCO.

A variety of additional provisions are expected to expand existing crop insurance products or require examination of the potential for new products, including those that would benefit specialty crops and animal agriculture. Provisions revise the value of crop insurance for organic crops to reflect generally higher prices of organic (not conventional) crops. USDA is also required to conduct more research on whole farm revenue insurance with higher coverage levels than currently available. Studies or policies are also required for insuring (1) specialty crop producers for food safety and contamination-related losses, (2) swine producers for a catastrophic disease event, (3) producers of catfish against reduction in the margin between the market prices and production costs, (4) commercial poultry production against business disruptions caused by integrator bankruptcy, (5) poultry producers for a catastrophic event, (6) producers of biomass sorghum or sweet sorghum grown as feedstock for renewable energy, and (7) alfalfa producers. A peanut revenue insurance product and rice margin insurance also are mandated. Another provision provides funding for index weather insurance for protecting against weather.

To address conservation concerns, the 2014 farm bill links eligibility for crop insurance premium subsidies to compliance with wetland and conservation requirements for highly erodible land. Also, crop insurance subsidies are reduced for plantings on native sod acreage in certain states.

In total, the crop insurance title increases funding for crop insurance by an additional $5.7 billion over 10 years relative to projected levels that assumed no change in policy. The largest cost items are for STAX ($3.3 billion) and SCO ($1.7 billion), according to the Congressional Budget Office. A controversial item not included in P.L. 113-79 was the reduction of premium subsidies for high-income farmers, which had been included in the Senate farm bill but not the House bill.

INTRODUCTION

The federal crop insurance program is considered by many farmers and policy makers as the centerpiece of the farm safety net. The program makes available subsidized insurance policies for about 130 commodities ranging from apples to wheat. These "multiple peril" policies help producers manage financial risks associated with crop yield or revenue losses. Insurable causes of losses include adverse weather (e.g., drought and flood), insects or disease outbreaks, and failure of irrigation water supply.

The enacted 2014 farm bill (the Agricultural Act of 2014; P.L. 113-79) enhances the federal crop insurance program by expanding its scope, covering a greater share of farm losses, and making a variety of other modifications that broaden policy coverage. This report describes in detail changes made to the program as part of the 2014 farm bill. A table at the end of this report (*Table A-1*) provides a side-by-side comparison of the crop insurance provisions in Title XI of the 2014 farm bill and the permanent authorizing statute for federal crop insurance (Federal Crop Insurance Act, 7 U.S.C. §1501 et seq.), prior to enactment of the 2014 farm bill.

Two other key elements of the farm safety net are (1) the farm commodity programs, which provide price and income support for a much narrower list of "covered and loan commodities" such as corn, soybeans, wheat, rice, and peanuts; and (2) agricultural disaster programs, which primarily assist producers owning livestock or fruit trees.

CROP INSURANCE BACKGROUND[1]

Policy Rationale for Federal Crop Insurance

In 1938, Congress established the federal crop insurance program following several unsuccessful attempts by the private sector to sell multiple-peril policies, beginning in the late 1800s.[2] These ventures lost money and were discontinued because areas they covered were too small to adequately distribute risks when crops failed. Since then, private crop insurance has focused on single peril insurance for causes of loss not correlated across wide areas, such as hail or fire.[3]

Agricultural weather risks typically affect a large area rather than individual farms, resulting in potential losses that historically have been considered too large for private insurers. Others, though, contend that international financial markets have expanded dramatically in recent decades and now have significant capacity to provide coverage of risks that are much greater than those associated with potential crop losses.[4]

Separately, the crop insurance program must address problems associated with moral hazard, such as farmers intentionally under-applying crop inputs to collect indemnities. Another issue is adverse selection, whereby high-risk farmers tend to participate more than low-risk farmers, thus increasing program costs. Some argue that the government is in a better position than the private sector to address these issues and monitor farm behavior and losses given better access to data and linkages with farm program benefits.

From a demand standpoint, federal subsidies for purchasing crop insurance have been increased over the years to improve affordability and boost farmer participation.[5] In general, the premium required to cover the cost of crop insurance is more than producers are willing to pay. As a result, in the absence of federal subsidies, U.S. agricultural acreage covered by crop insurance and coverage levels selected by farmers would likely be lower, potentially increasing the odds of a costly federal bailout in the event of a catastrophic weather event.

Proponents of federal crop insurance argue that the program is essential because it provides specific risk management solutions that benefit farmers, input suppliers, the entire agricultural sector, and ultimately all food consumers. They also say widespread participation reduces the potential for ad-hoc disaster spending, a longstanding policy goal. In contrast, critics argue that the program covers an excessive amount of producer risk, inappropriately subsidizes large farms, wastes taxpayer dollars, and encourages crop production on environmentally fragile lands.

Authorizing Legislation

The federal crop insurance program is permanently authorized by the Federal Crop Insurance Act, as amended (7 U.S.C. §1501 et seq.). The Federal Crop Insurance Corporation (FCIC) was created as a wholly-owned government corporation in 1938 to carry out the program. The program is administered by the U.S. Department of Agriculture's Risk Management Agency (RMA).

Insurable Commodities and Types of Policies

Policies are available for approximately 130 crops and cover more than 250 million acres nationwide. Insurable commodities include major field crops such as wheat, corn, soybeans, cotton, peanuts, and rice, as well as many specialty crops (including fruit, tree nut, vegetable, and nursery crops), pasture, rangeland, and forage crops.[6] For major crops, three-fourths or more of U.S. planted acreage is insured under the federal crop insurance program.

Farmers annually purchase about 1.2 million policies, with many producers purchasing multiple policies depending on farm size and number of crops grown. The policies protect against individual farm losses in yield, crop revenue, or whole farm revenue. Area-wide policies are available for some crops, whereby an indemnity is paid when there is an overall loss over a broad area level. In general, yield-based policies offer a guarantee at the individual farm level or area-wide (e.g., county) level. For revenue policies, the insurance guarantee also incorporates the expected market price prior to planting (i.e., no statutory minimum prices as provided in some farm programs). For some policies, the guarantee can increase if the harvest price is higher than the expected price, thereby increasing the point at which indemnities are triggered.

The producer selects a coverage level and absorbs the initial loss through the deductible. For example, a coverage level of 70% has a 30% deductible (for a total equal to 100% of the expected value prior to planting the crop). The producer pays a portion of the premium which increases as the level of coverage rises. The federal government pays the rest of the premium—62%, on average, in 2013—plus the cost of selling and servicing the policies. This differs from farm commodity programs, which require no participation fees. Also unlike farm commodity programs, crop insurance has no subsidy limits, and participants can be eligible regardless of income levels.

Program Structure and Federal Costs

The federal crop insurance program is a partnership between RMA (through the FCIC) and private industry. RMA approves and supports products, develops and approves the premium rates, administers premium subsidies, reimburses private companies for their administrative and operating costs (i.e., delivery costs for selling and servicing the policies), and reinsures company losses. RMA also sponsors educational and outreach programs and seminars on the general topic of risk management.

Approximately 19 private insurance companies provide the "boots on the ground" for selling and servicing the insurance policies through a network of agents. They also share risk (profit/loss potential) with the government. The Standard Reinsurance Agreement (SRA) defines the risk-sharing arrangement, whereby insurance companies may transfer some liability associated with riskier policies to the federal government and retain profits/losses from less risky policies.[7]

During FY2009-FY2013, federal costs averaged $8.4 billion per year, varying between $3.7 billion in FY2010 and $14.1 billion in FY2012, depending on crop losses and commodity prices, which affect premium subsidy amounts and program liability (e.g., high market price result in high premiums and liability).

CROP INSURANCE PROVISIONS IN THE 2014 FARM BILL

The general enhancement of the federal crop insurance program in the 2014 farm bill stems from the desire of many in Congress, particularly members of the agriculture committees, to bolster what they consider to be the most significant aspect of the farm safety net. Unlike farm commodity programs, federal crop insurance is applicable to a wide variety of crops and requires producers to pay for at least part of the program. Producers are indemnified only after an insurable crop loss. During the farm bill debate, some in Congress voiced concerns that the program is too generous. Congress considered but did not pass premium caps and/or income limits on crop insurance similar to ones governing farm commodity program payments.

For crop insurance in the 2014 farm bill, a prominent feature is the authorization of policies designed to reimburse "shallow losses"—an insured producer's out-of-pocket loss associated with the policy deductible. These include a new crop insurance policy called Stacked Income Protection Plan (STAX) for upland cotton and the Supplemental Coverage Option (SCO) for other crops. A variety of additional provisions are expected to expand existing crop insurance products or require FCIC to examine the potential for new products, including those benefiting specialty crops and animal agriculture.

Stacked Income Protection Plan (STAX) for Upland Cotton

Beginning with the 2014 farm bill, upland cotton is no longer a "covered commodity," making upland cotton producers ineligible for either Price Loss Coverage (PLC) or Agriculture Risk Coverage (ARC) under the farm commodity support programs. Instead, upland cotton is eligible for Stacked Income Protection (STAX), which is a revenue-based, area-wide crop insurance policy that may be purchased as a stand-alone policy for primary coverage or purchased in tandem with an individual farm loss policy or area policy. This major policy revision was sought by U.S. cotton producers in an attempt to resolve a long-running trade dispute with Brazil that requires changing the U.S. cotton support program so it does not distort international markets.[8]

Critical to participation, and as part of the agreement to make upland cotton ineligible for the PLC/ARC programs, is the government's share of the premium cost. The federal subsidy is 80% for STAX and the government pays for delivery costs. Policies are to be offered in all producing counties at the county level, or on the basis of a larger geographic area if necessary. A payment rate multiplier of 120% is available if producers want to increase the amount of protection per acre.

The indemnity from STAX is triggered by a revenue loss at the county level. When purchased as a "stacked" policy, the indemnity is designed to cover part of the deductible of the underlying policy. Specifically, STAX would indemnify losses in county revenue of greater than 10% of expected revenue but not more than 30%.[9] For producers purchasing STAX in conjunction with an individual policy, the maximum coverage under STAX cannot exceed the deductible level selected by the producer in the underlying individual policy. For individual producers, indemnities for STAX and other policies cannot overlap.

A graphical illustration of STAX is shown *Figure 1*. The bar on the left depicts the expected revenue (prior to planting) under a typical cotton crop insurance revenue policy with a 30% deductible (the farmer absorbs the first 30% of the loss). The expected revenue is the 10-year average yield for an individual producer times the expected market price (the average futures market price prior to planting). The insurance guarantee is set at 70% of the expected revenue (100% minus the 30% deductible). Upon harvest, if actual revenue falls short of the guarantee, an initial indemnity is triggered under the farmer's individual crop insurance policy as depicted by the green box in the right-hand column. If a STAX policy is also purchased and there is a loss at the county level, a STAX indemnity would be paid (depicted by the blue box). Overall, the farmer incurs a loss of approximately 10% (white box at top), with the STAX indemnity reducing the amount of "shallow loss" absorbed by the producer.

(STAX for upland cotton covers part of the deductible under the individual policy)

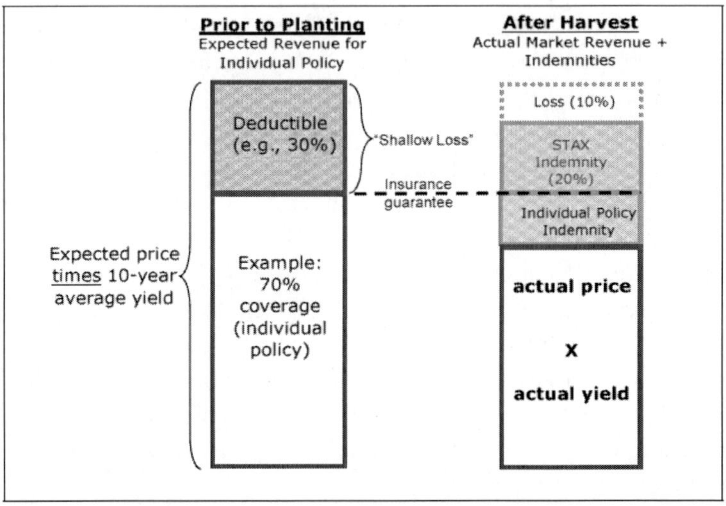

Source: CRS.

Notes: A STAX indemnity (blue box above) is triggered when actual county revenue is less than 90% of expected county revenue. Scenario assumes expected (and actual) revenue is the same at the individual farm and county level (STAX). STAX may be purchased as a stand-alone policy for primary coverage. Upland cotton acres enrolled in STAX are not eligible for SCO.

Figure 1. Stacked Income Protection Plan (STAX) with a Crop Loss.

Supplemental Coverage Option (SCO)

Like STAX but for other crops, the Supplemental Coverage Option (SCO) is authorized by the 2014 farm bill to cover part of the deductible under the producer's underlying policy (the "shallow loss"). SCO is an area-wide (e.g., county) loss policy, whereby an indemnity is paid on area losses not more than the deductible level (e.g., 25%) selected by the producer for the underlying individual policy. However, unlike STAX, the SCO guarantee can be based on either expected county yields or revenue, and it must be purchased in conjunction with a traditional crop insurance policy. Indemnities are triggered by county losses greater than 14%, and policy coverage cannot exceed the difference between 86% and the coverage level selected by the producer for the underlying policy.

A graphical illustration of SCO is shown in *Figure 2*.[10] The bar on the left depicts the expected revenue (prior to planting) under a typical crop insurance revenue policy with a 30% deductible (the farmer absorbs the first 30% of the loss). The expected revenue is the 10-year average yield for a producer times the expected market price (e.g., average futures market price for major crops). The guarantee is set at 70% of the expected revenue (100% minus the 30% deductible). If a loss occurs on the farm, an initial indemnity is triggered under the farmer's individual crop insurance policy as depicted by the green box in the right-hand column. If an SCO policy is also purchased and there is also a loss at the county level, a indemnity from the SCO also would be paid (depicted by the blue box). Overall, the farmer incurs a loss of approximately 14% (white box at top), with the SCO indemnity reducing the "shallow loss" absorbed by the producer.

(SCO covers part of the deductible under the individual policy)

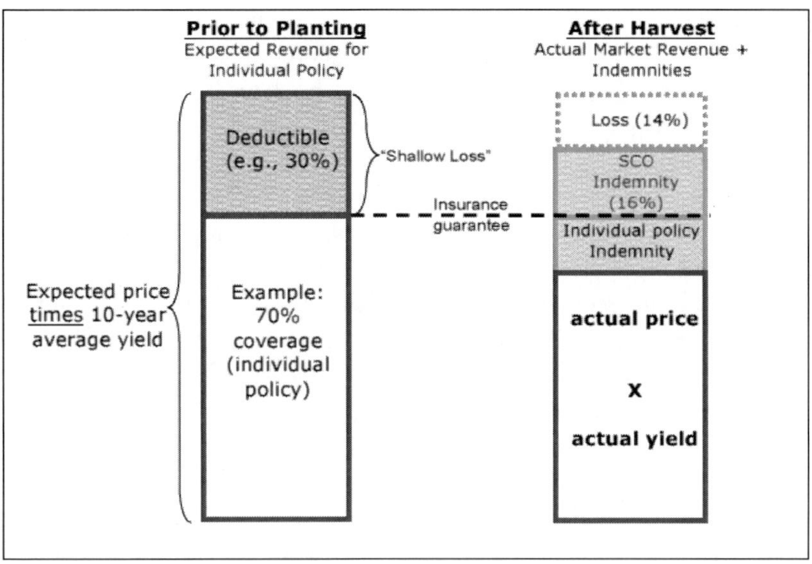

Source: CRS.

Notes: SCO indemnity (in blue box above) is triggered by a loss in county revenue (or yield if underlying individual policy is yield-based). Scenario assumes expected (and actual) revenue is the same at the individual farm and county level (SCO).

Figure 2. Supplemental Coverage Option (SCO) with a Crop Loss.

SCO is designed to serve as a "shallow loss" program for covered commodities enrolled by producers in Price Loss Coverage (PLC) under the farm commodity support program. A separate PLC payment would be made if the farm price for the crop is below a "reference price" set in statute. For crops enrolled in the alternative Agriculture Risk Coverage (ARC) program, SCO is not available because ARC is already designed to pay for "shallow losses."[11]

SCO policies are to be offered for crops that have sufficient data for policy development, and coverage is to begin no later than the 2015 crop year. USDA has announced plans for developing 2015 policies for corn, grain sorghum, rice, soybeans, winter wheat, spring wheat, and cotton.[12] The government subsidy as a share of the policy premium is 65%.

"Enterprise Units" and Yield Guarantees

Currently available policies are enhanced through a number of provisions beginning with the 2015 crop year. To provide better coverage for producers with both irrigated and nonirrigated crops, separate insurable "enterprise" units for each practice will be available (an enterprise unit is all land for a single crop in a county, regardless of the tenant/landlord structure). Separating the acreage can increase risk protection for producers because losses on dryland crops would no longer be offset by higher yields on irrigated acreage when the two are combined.

Another concern of producers in recent years has been the treatment of poor yields used to establish the insurance guarantee, which is based on 4 to 10 years of historical yields called actual production history (APH). Current law allows a "yield plug" if the producer's actual or appraised yield for any particularly year is less than 60% of the "transitional yield," generally based on the 10-year historical county average yield. The yield plug allows the replacement of a low actual yield in the APH with a yield equal to 60% of the applicable transitional yield. The 2014 farm bill enhances this provision by keeping the yield plug unchanged from current law (except in the case of native sod) but allowing producers to exclude without replacement any recorded or appraised yield from the APH calculation if the average crop yield in the county for any particular year is less than 50% of the 10-year county average.

Peanuts and Rice

The peanut and rice industries successfully argued for enhanced crop insurance options. The 2014 farm bill mandates a peanut revenue insurance product and rice margin insurance, with both to be made available for the 2015 crop year. For several years, rice producers have been interested in protecting against rising cost of inputs (e.g., fuel, fertilizer) as it affects their margin (income minus costs). For peanut producers, the revenue policy is to use the "Rotterdam price index" or other appropriate prices as determined by the Secretary. Setting the price guarantee is problematic for peanuts because the market is considered "thin," with only two peanut shellers reportedly buying over 80% of all peanuts from growers. No futures market exists for peanuts, and private contracts between producers and shellers reportedly account for most transactions, making it difficult to independently verify pricing needed to help set price parameters in the insurance policies.

Alfalfa and Industrial Crops

The 2014 farm bill also requires FCIC to enter into contracts to conduct research and development on modifications to insurance currently available for alfalfa through the "forage production" policy. Geographic coverage of the existing policy is limited, and supporters of the provision have said that loss coverage has been inadequate.

FCIC is also to research policies for crops currently not insurable, including biomass sorghum and sweet sorghum grown expressly for the purpose of producing a feedstock for renewable biofuel, renewable electricity, or biobased products.

Provisions for Specialty Crop Producers

Federal crop insurance is available for over 80 specialty crops (including fruit, tree nut, vegetable, and nursery crops), making the program the primary financial safety net for specialty crop producers. While additional policies have been introduced over the last 10 years, producer groups and some Members of Congress during the farm bill debate wanted to improve the safety net for specialty crops, in part since these crops are not eligible for farm commodity support programs.

Whole Farm Insurance

USDA is required to conduct more research on whole farm revenue insurance with higher coverage levels than currently available under the Adjusted Gross Revenue (AGR) and AGR-Lite policies which insure revenue of the entire farm rather than an individual crop.[13] In general, the AGR products are designed to protect producers with specialty crops and/or commodities not covered by individual policies. Historically, whole-farm insurance has seen limited participation, in part because the products are complex, the policies are available only in some parts of the country, and the maximum available coverage of 80% is considered too low for adequate risk protection.

FCIC has been working on a revised whole farm insurance plan that reportedly reflects provisions on whole farm insurance specified in the 2014 farm bill. The farm bill provisions include increasing available coverage from 80% to 85%, and a maximum liability of $1.5 million, up from $1 million for AGR-Lite. Also, eligible producers are to include direct-to-consumer marketers and producers who produce multiple agricultural commodities, including specialty crops, industrial crops, livestock, and aquaculture products. FCIC also may provide diversification-based additional coverage payment rates, premium discounts, or other enhanced benefits in recognition of the risk management benefits of crop and livestock diversification strategies for producers. FCIC can also expand coverage for the value of any packing, packaging, or any other similar on-farm activity that FCIC determines to be the minimum required in order to remove the commodity from the field.

Organic Prices for Insuring Crops

Current law requires FCIC to broaden coverage for organic crops. To reflect the higher product value and provide additional protection for producers, organic price elections have been made available for 16 crops as of early 2014. The 2014 farm bill extends the current practice by requiring FCIC to offer price elections by 2015 that reflect actual retail or wholesale prices of organic (not conventional) crops for all organic crops produced in compliance with standards issued by USDA under the Organic Foods Production Act of 1990.

"NAP" Enhancement

When crop insurance is not available, catastrophic coverage under the existing noninsured crop disaster assistance program (NAP) can be purchased from USDA's Farm Service Agency. NAP applicants pay an administrative fee (currently $250 per crop), and no premium is charged (like CAT crop insurance). In order to receive a NAP payment, a producer must experience at least a 50% crop loss caused by a natural disaster, or be prevented from planting more than 35% of intended crop acreage. For production losses in excess of the minimum, a producer receives 55% of the average market price for the commodity.

In order to expand coverage for specialty crops and others covered under NAP, the 2014 farm bill provides additional coverage at 50% to 65% of established yield and 100% of average market price. The farmer-paid premium for additional coverage is 5.25% times the product of the selected coverage level and value of production (acreage times yield times average market price). Also, the per-person payment limit is increased from $100,000 to $125,000. Separately, to assist producers with fruit crop losses in 2012, payments associated with additional coverage are made retroactively (minus premium fees) in counties declared a disaster due to freeze or frost.

Index-based Weather Insurance

FCIC is authorized to conduct two or more pilot programs (and approve subsequent policies) for index-based weather insurance. Index weather insurance protects against specific weather events and not actual losses. Priority is given to specialty crops (e.g., fruits and vegetables) and livestock commodities (including pasture, rangeland, and forage) that have had no available coverage or have low participation rates under existing coverage. The subsidy shall not exceed 60% of the estimated premium amount. Administrative and operating expenses are to be reimbursed as with other policies, but federal reinsurance, research and development costs, and other reimbursements or maintenance fees are not provided for these policies. Expenditures from the FCIC fund are limited to $12.5 million per year for FY2015-2018.

Policies may be sold by the approved insurance provider that submits the application as well as others who agree to pay maintenance fees to the submitting provider. Policies cannot be substantially similar to privately available hail insurance.

Food Safety Insurance Study

The 2014 farm bill requires FCIC to contract for a study on coverage for specialty crops that would indemnify producers for production or revenue losses related to food safety concerns such as government, retail, or national consumer group announcements of a health advisory, product removal, or recall related to a contamination concern. FCIC must submit a report to Congress within one year of enactment of the farm bill.

Studies for Animal Agriculture Insurance

Compared with the crop sector, the federal crop insurance program provides only limited coverage for the livestock industry. Relatively new or pilot programs protect livestock and dairy producers from loss of gross margin or price declines. Livestock producers can also insure against hay and forage losses through the Forage Production policy (see "Alfalfa and Industrial Crops" above) and the Pasture, Rangeland, and Forage program, which uses a rainfall index or vegetative index to determine loss.

The 2014 farm bill directs FCIC to study a variety of topics that could lead to additional insurance policies for animal agriculture. FCIC is required to enter into contracts to conduct research and development on policies for the margin between the market value of catfish and input costs and poultry business interruption insurance for poultry growers, including losses due to bankruptcy of an integrator (owner-processor). FCIC is also required to contract for studies on insuring swine producers for a catastrophic event and insuring poultry producers for a catastrophic event.

Conservation Provisions

As directed in the conservation title (II) of the 2014 farm bill, crop insurance premium subsidies are available only if producers are in compliance with wetland conservation requirements and conservation requirements for highly erodible land. USDA expects most producers will be unaffected because the same requirement has been in place for years to maintain eligibility for farm program and other USDA benefits.

Also, to limit the incentive to convert native sod to cropland, a separate provision in the crop insurance title affects producers purchasing policies for crop insurance or noninsured crop disaster assistance program (NAP). For the first four years of planting on native sod acreage in Iowa, Minnesota, Montana, Nebraska, North Dakota, and South Dakota, farmers will pay more for the risk coverage through reduced crop insurance subsidies or higher NAP fees, and the yield guarantee is reduced compared to other cropland. For details, see *Table A-1*.

Provisions for Beginning Farmers

To help develop the next generation of producers, the 2014 farm bill makes several changes to benefit beginning farmers or ranchers with less than five years of experience. For example, to reduce the cost of purchasing crop insurance for beginning farmers or ranchers, the $300 fee for purchasing catastrophic (CAT) coverage is waived. Also, the premium subsidy schedule for additional coverage is increased by 10 percentage points.

To boost the yield guarantee for beginning farmers, the calculation can now use yields recorded by prior producers on the acreage, which might be higher than the alternative when historical data are not available (i.e., 65% of the transitional yield based on county average yields). When historical data are available to establish the producer's actual production history, beginning farmers can replace low yields with a yield equal to 80% of the transitional yield.

Similar benefits are provided under the noninsured crop disaster assistance program (NAP), which provides catastrophic coverage for uninsurable crops. The provision extends the fee waiver for basic NAP coverage to beginning farmers and socially disadvantaged farmers. Premium for additional NAP coverage is reduced by 50% for limited resource, beginning, and socially disadvantaged farmers.[14]

"Budget Neutral" for the Next Standard Reinsurance Agreement

As authorized by the 2008 farm bill, the Federal Crop Insurance Corporation (FCIC) negotiated with private companies to revise the Standard Reinsurance Agreement (SRA) to save federal money and improve program delivery in underserved areas. The SRA, in place since 2011, governs the terms under which the government pays participating insurance companies to sell and service policies and shares underwriting gains or losses with them. The changes made in 2011 put a cap on administrative and operating (A&O) costs and limited agent commissions, measures opposed by the crop insurance companies. Some but not all of the estimated $6 billion in budget savings over 10 years was reinvested back into crop insurance, including expansion of the Pasture, Rangeland, and Forage crop insurance program. FCIC may renegotiate the SRA once every five years.

To ensure that insurance companies are not adversely affected by changes in the next SRA, the 2014 farm bill requires that any revised SRA is budget neutral with respect to estimates of future underwriting gains for the private companies, and the estimated total A&O reimbursements cannot be less than the amounts that would have been provided under the previous SRA. The Manager's Report states their intent is that a renegotiated SRA should not be used as a means of achieving further cuts in the federal crop insurance program. During the farm bill debate, some Members of Congress argued that such cuts, if any, should be made by Congress so it could claim the budget savings towards either deficit reduction or to offset the cost of any new legislative initiative.

Premium Subsidies

Unlike farm commodity programs, the federal crop insurance program does not have an income limit test for program eligibility or premium subsidy limits. The topic was widely discussed in Congress during the farm bill debate, particularly in 2012 and 2013.

A controversial item not included in P.L. 113-79 was the reduction of premium subsidies for high income farmers, a provision that was included in the Senate bill but not the House bill. In the 2012 farm bill passed by the Senate in the 112th Congress, an amendment was adopted during floor debate to reduce crop insurance premium subsidies by 15 percentage points for producers with average adjusted gross income greater than $750,000. In 2013, the Senate Agriculture Committee-reported version of S. 954 did not include the provision, but an amendment to S. 954 requiring the subsidy reduction was adopted on the Senate floor in June 2013 by a vote of 59-33. A House amendment to limit crop insurance premium subsidies failed during floor debate in June 2013.[15]

ESTIMATED COST OF THE CROP INSURANCE TITLE

Prior to enactment of the 2014 farm bill, projected baseline expenditures for the federal crop insurance program were estimated at $84.1 billion over 10 years, according to the Congressional Budget Office. The enacted 2014 farm bill (P.L. 113-79) increased expected outlays for crop insurance relative to this 10-year baseline level by an additional $5.7 billion (*Table 1*).

Table 1. Cost of Provisions in the Crop Insurance Title of the 2014 Farm Bill (in millions of dollars)

Description	5 years: FY2014-FY2018	10 years: FY2014-FY2023
CBO baseline, May 2013, Crop Insurance	39,592	84,105
CBO score of changes in Title XI (Crop Insurance) of the 2014 farm bill		
Provisions with net savings:		
Premium amounts for catastrophic (CAT) crop insurance	-153	-426
Crop production on native sod	-34	-114
Participation effects of commodity programs[a]	-240	-464
Provisions with net additional costs:		
Supplemental Coverage Option (SCO)	544	1,716
Crop margin coverage	15	40
Enterprise units for irrigated and nonirrigated crops	188	533
Adjustment in actual producer history (APH) yields	120	357
Coverage level by practice	60	168
Beginning farmer and rancher provisions	84	261
Stacked Income Protection (STAX) for cotton	1,054	3,288
Peanut revenue crop insurance	44	119
Implementation	55	70
Crop insurance fraud	36	81
Research and development priorities	16	36
Crop Insurance for organic crops	3	8
Index-based weather insurance	37	50
Subtotal: CBO Score of 2014 Farm Bill changes, Title XI	1,828	5,722
CBO Estimate of Total Cost of Crop Insurance	41,420	89,827

Source: CBO baseline and score of the conference agreement of H.R. 2642, the Agricultural Act of 2014, as reported on January 27, 2014.

Notes: Changes to the noninsured crop assistance program (NAP) in Title XII are estimated to increase outlays by $159 million during 2014-2018 and $226 million during 2014-2023.

[a] Producers are expected to purchase less crop insurance (which reduces federal costs) when participating in the Agricultural Risk Coverage (ARC) program authorized in Title I.

The largest cost items are the Stacked Income Protection (STAX) for cotton, estimated at $3.3 billion over 10 years, and the Supplemental Coverage Option (SCO), estimated at $1.7 billion over 10 years. Several general enhancements involve expanded coverage for irrigated crops and revising yield history for setting yield guarantees. The combined cost of these upgrades is more than $1 billion over 10 years.

The largest cost savings item for Title XI relates to the interaction between crop insurance and farm programs authorized in Title I. The Agricultural Risk Coverage (ARC) program is designed to cover some losses that crop insurance might otherwise cover. Therefore, producers who enroll their crop in ARC might purchase reduced coverage levels for crop insurance, which would reduce federal expenditures on total premium subsidies and administrative and operating costs.

APPENDIX. CROP INSURANCE PROVISIONS IN THE ENACTED 2014 FARM BILL

Table A-1. Crop Insurance Provisions in the Enacted 2014 Farm Bill Compared with Previous Law

Previous Law/Policy	2014 Farm Bill (P.L. 113-79)
Information Sharing and Publication of Violations	
USDA, an approved insurance provider and its employees and contractors, and any other person may not disclose to the public information furnished by a producer unless it has been aggregated to avoid disclosure of an individual's information. *[7 U.S.C. 1502(c)]*	Adds provision that, if authorized by a producer, USDA's Farm Service Agency is to provide to an insurance agent or approved insurance provider any information or maps that may assist the agent or provider insuring the producer. *[Sec. 11001]*
Adjustments to producer premiums are prohibited as an inducement to purchase crop insurance, with few exceptions. *[7 U.S.C. 1508(a)(9)]*	To deter potential violators, the Federal Crop Insurance Corporation (FCIC) is required to publish in detail (but without disclosing identities) any violations of the existing prohibition on adjustments to premiums, including sanctions imposed. *[Sec. 11002]*
Supplemental Coverage Option (SCO)	
No comparable provision.	Makes available to crop producers a policy called Supplemental Coverage Option (SCO) to cover part of the deductible under the producer's underlying policy. SCO is an area-wide (e.g., county) yield or revenue loss policy, whereby an indemnity is paid on

Previous Law/Policy	2014 Farm Bill (P.L. 113-79)
	area losses not more than the deductible level (e.g., 25%) selected by the producer for the underlying individual policy. Coverage is triggered by losses greater than 14%, and policy coverage cannot exceed the difference between 86% and the coverage level selected by the producer for the underlying policy. Acres covered by Agriculture Risk Coverage (ARC) or STAX (see below) are not eligible for SCO. SCO policies are to be made available for all crops if sufficient data are available. Premium subsidized at 65%. Coverage to begin no later than the 2015 crop year. *[Sec. 11003]* A crop margin coverage option is available as a single policy or in combination with a yield or revenue loss policy. *[Sec. 11004]*
Catastrophic Yield Policies (CAT)	
Catastrophic yield policies (CAT) are available for yield losses greater than 50%. Premium is fully subsidized, and producer pays an administrative fee of $300 per crop per county. Participating crop insurance companies are reimbursed for selling and servicing the policies based on the premium amount. *[7 U.S.C. 1508(d)(2)]*	CAT remains fully subsidized, and reimbursements to private insurance companies remain tied to the calculated premium. To reduce government costs of reimbursement, the calculated premium is reduced by the percentage equal to the difference between the average loss ratio (premiums divided by indemnities times 100) for the crop and 100%, plus a reasonable reserve as determined by FCIC. *[Sec. 11005]* In Title XII—Miscellaneous: Prohibits CAT coverage on crops and grasses used for grazing. *[Sec. 12305(b)]*
Enterprise and Whole Farm Units	
Crops are insured based on geographic units defined in the insurance policy. The basic unit covers land in one county with the same tenant/landlord. An optional unit is a basic unit divided into smaller units by township section. An enterprise unit covers all land of a single crop in a county for a producer, regardless of tenant/landlord structure. A whole farm unit covers more than one crop. For a policy with an enterprise or whole farm unit paragraph, *on a pilot basis,* the	The subsidy for enterprise and whole farm units is made permanent (previously apilot basis). *[Sec. 11006]* Beginning with the 2015 crop year, separate enterprise units will be available for irrigated and nonirrigated acreages of crops. *[Sec. 11007]*

Table A-1. (Continued)

Previous Law/Policy	2014 Farm Bill (P.L. 113-79)
percentage of the premium paid by the government shall provide the same dollar amount of premium subsidy per acre as for other units, up to 80%. *[7 U.S.C. 1508(e)(5)]*	
Data Collection for Yield Guarantees; Yield Adjustments	
FCIC bases policy guarantees on a producer's actual production history (APH) for the crop, or on county yields for area-wide policies. The APH is based on producer yields for the prior 4 to 10 years. *[7 U.S.C. 1508(g)(2)]*	Specifically directs FCIC to use county data collected by USDA's Risk Management Agency and/or National Agricultural Statistics Service. If such data are not available, it may use other data considered appropriate by the Secretary of Agriculture. *[Sec.11008]*
If, for one or more of the crop years used to establish the producer's actual production history (APH) of an agricultural commodity, the producer's recorded or appraised yield of the commodity was less than 60% of the applicable transitional yield (based on 10-year historical county average yield), FCIC can at the election of the producer exclude the recorded or appraised yield and replace it with a yield equal to 60% of the applicable transitional yield. Concept is known as yield substitution with a "yield plug." *[7 U.S.C. 1508(g)(4)(B)]*	Yield plug remains unchanged from current law but producers may elect to exclude any recorded or appraised yield from the APH calculation if the crop yield in the county is less than 50% of the 10-year county average. Separate determinations are made for irrigated and nonirrigated acreage. Producers in contiguous (adjacent) counties can do the same. *[Sec. 11009]*
Policy Research Development, Review, Approval, and Cost Reimbursement	
An approved insurance provider, a college or university, a cooperative or trade association, or others may prepare for submission or propose to FCIC crop insurance policies and provisions of policies. *[7 U.S.C. 1508(h)(1)]* Under sections 522 and 523 of the Federal Crop Insurance Act, FCIC may enter into contracts to carry out research and development for new crop insurance policies (but may not conduct research itself). FCIC shall establish as one of the highest research priorities the development of a pasture, range, and forage program. It shall provide a	ddsrequirement that FCIC must review and submit to the FCIC Board any policy developed under section 522(c) or pilot program developed under section 523 if FCIC determines that it will likely result in (i) a viable and marketable policy, (ii) would provide crop insurance coverage in a significantly improved form, and (iii) adequately protects the interests of producers. Also, the Board shall review and approve for sale a new policy if the Board determines: (i) the interests of producers are adequately protected, (ii) the proposed policy will: (I)

Previous Law/Policy	2014 Farm Bill (P.L. 113-79)
payment to an applicant for research and development costs. *[7 U.S.C. 1522]*	provide a new kind of coverage that is likely to be viable and marketable; (II) provide crop insurance coverage in a manner that addresses a clear and identifiable flaw or problem in an existing policy; or (III) provide a new kind of coverage for a commodity that previously had no available crop insurance, or has demonstrated a low level of participation or coverage level under existing coverage; and (iii) the proposed policy will not have a significant adverse impact on the crop insurance delivery system. The Board is to give first priority to new policies that address underserved commodities (limited or no available coverage), and then to existing policies for which there is inadequate coverage or there exists low levels of participation. Requires by the 2015 crop year a revenue policy for peanut producers and a margin coverage policy for rice producers. *[Sec. 11010(a)]*
The Board may approve up to 50% of the projected total research and development costs to be paid in advance to an applicant if it determines that: (i) the concept will likely result in a viable and marketable policy consistent with section 1508(h) of this title; (ii) in the sole opinion of the Board, the concept would provide crop insurance coverage-(I) in a significantly improved form; (II) to a crop or region not traditionally served by the federal crop insurance program; or (III) in a form that addresses a recognized flaw or problem in the program; (iii) the applicant agrees to provide such reports as FCIC determines are necessary to monitor the development effort; (iv) the proposed budget and timetable are reasonable; and (v) the concept proposal meets any other requirements that the Board determines appropriate. *[7 U.S.C. 1522(b)(2)]*	Same as current law and authorizes Board to waive the 50% limitation and approve an additional 25% advance payment if the intended policy will provide coverage for a region or crop that is underserved by the federal crop insurance program, including specialty crops, and the submitter is making satisfactory progress towards developing a viable and marketable policy. *[Sec. 11010(b)]*

Table A-1. (Continued)

Previous Law/Policy	2014 Farm Bill (P.L. 113-79)
A private sector entity can propose an insurance plan to be added to the FCIC portfolio of products. A process must be established to review and approve products. *[7 U.S.C. 1508(h)(4)]*	As part of the submission process for policies involving fruits and vegetables, tree nuts, dried fruits, and horticulture and nursery crops (including floriculture), the applicant must consult with producer groups potentially affected. Any submission must contain a summary of these findings. FCIC shall determine if the policy will create adverse market distortions. *[Sec. 11011]*
Standard Reinsurance Agreement and Risk-Sharing	
The Standard Reinsurance Agreement (SRA) between FCIC and private companies defines expense reimbursements and risk-sharing by the government, including the terms under which the government provides subsidies and reinsurance (i.e., insurance for insurance companies) on eligible crop insurance contracts sold or reinsured by insurance companies. FCIC may renegotiate the SRA once every 5 years. *[7 U.S.C. 1508(k)(8)]*	Any renegotiated SRA is to be budget neutral with respect to underwriting gains. Also, estimated reimbursement for administrative and operating (A&O) costs cannot be less than the amounts under the immediately preceding SRA if it were extended. Any budget savings from a renegotiated SRA shall be used to increase underwriting gains or A&O reimbursements. *[Sec. 11012]*
Corn with Low Test	
Under an insurance policy, if an agricultural commodity does not meet established quality standards, actual production (used for determining the indemnity) is reduced accordingly. *[7 U.S.C. 1508(m)]*	FCIC shall establish procedures to allow insured producers not more than 120 days to settle claims involving corn that is determined to have low test weight. FCIC is to implement this provision on a regional basis based on market conditions and the interests of producers. Authority for this provision terminates 5 years after implementation. *[Sec. 11013]*
Crop Production on Native Sod ("Sod Saver") and Conservation Compliance Sod Saver: Subject to a geographic condition below, native sod planted to an insurable crop (over 5 acres) is ineligible for crop insurance and the noninsured crop disaster assistance program (NAP) for the first 5 years of planting. May apply to virgin prairie converted to cropland only in the Prairie Pothole National Priority Area, if elected by	During the first 4 years of planting, crop insurance and NAP benefits are reduced on native sod acreage in Minnesota, Iowa, North Dakota, South Dakota, Montana, and Nebraska. Provisions include: (1) a reduction in the crop insurance premium subsidy by 50 percentage points, and NAP fee is doubled; (2) annual data for APH are equal to 65% of the transitional yield for all four years rather than the higher, variable

Previous Law/Policy	2014 Farm Bill (P.L. 113-79)
the state. *[7 U.S.C. 1508(o)]* and *[7 U.S.C. 7333(a)(4)]* To complete the actual production history (APH) database used for calculating the yield guarantee, a farmer can use a variable percentage of the transitional yield (Tyield), depending on the number of years of actual history: 1 year = 80%, 2 years =90%, 3 years =100%. *[p. 254 of the 2014 Crop Insurance Handbook, FCIC18010]* Yield substitutes are allowed. *[See above: 7 U.S.C. 1508(g)(4)(B)]*	percentage applicable for other cropland; and (3) for crop insurance, yield substitutes are not allowed; that is, low farm yields must be used in the APH rather than replacing them with potentially higher T-yields. (On other cropland, producers can substitute 60% of the T-yield for any actual yield below 60% of the T-yield). USDA is required to submit an annual report to Congress that describes cropland acreage in each applicable county and state, and the change in cropland acreage from the preceding year, beginning with calendar year 2000. *[Sec. 11014]*
Conservation Compliance: In exchange for certain USDA program benefits, including commodity support programs, conservation programs, disaster payments, and operating loans, a producer agrees to maintain a minimum level of conservation on highly erodible land. Highly erodible land can be considered eligible for program benefits if the land user agrees to cultivate the land using an approved conservation plan or qualifies for an exemption. *[16 U.S.C. 3811 et seq.]*	In Title II—Conservation: Adds the federally funded portion of crop insurance premiums to the list of program benefits that could be lost if a producer is found to produce an agricultural commodity on certain converted wetlands or highly erodible land without an approved conservation plan or qualifying exemption. Violation resulting in ineligibility for crop insurance subsidy payments applies to reinsurance years subsequent to the date of the final determination of a violation (including all appeals). *[Sec. 2611(a)]*
Coverage Levels by Practice	
No comparable provision.	Beginning with the 2015 crop year, a producer who grows a crop on both dry land and irrigated land may elect a different coverage level for each production practice. *[Sec. 11015]*
Provisions for Beginning Farmers and Ranchers	
For catastrophic risk protection (CAT), producers pay an administrative fee of $300 per crop per county. *[7 U.S.C. 1508(b)(5)(A)]* The fee is waived for limited resource farmers (defined by USDA as those who have farm sales not more than $172,800 and household income at or below the national poverty level for a family of four). *[7 U.S.C. 1508(b)(5)(E)]* Premium subsidies	"Beginning farmer or rancher' means a farmer or rancher who has not actively operated and managed a farm or ranch with a bona fide insurable interest in a crop or livestock as an owner-operator, landlord, tenant, or sharecropper for more than 5 crop years, The following is provided for beginning farmers or ranchers: (1) waiver of CAT fees, (2) premium assistance that is 10

Table A-1. (Continued)

Previous Law/Policy	2014 Farm Bill (P.L. 113-79)
for buy-up coverage (above CAT) depend on level of coverage. *[7 U.S.C. 1508(e)]* For producers without historical yield data, the assigned yield in yield coverage plans is not less than 65% of the transitional yield of the producer or as determined by FCIC. *[7 U.S.C. 1508(g)(2)(B)]* When FCIC uses the actual production records of the producer to establish the producer's actual production history, an individual year may be excluded from the yield history if the appraised yield is less than 60% of the transitional yield, and the excluded yield can be replaced with a yield equal to 60% of the transitional yield. *[7 U.S.C. 1508(g)(4)(B)(ii)]*	percentage points greater than general subsidy schedule, (3) in the absence of historical data, an assigned yield that can be based on the crop yields recorded by prior producers on the acreage, and (4) excluded yields can be replaced with a yield equal to 80% of the transitional yield. *[Sec. 11016]*
New Policies: Stacked Income Protection Plan (STAX) for Producers of Upland Cotton and Peanut Revenue Crop Insurance	
No comparable provision.	Beginning with the 2015 crop, the FCIC shall make available to producers of upland cotton the Stacked Income Protection Plan (STAX), which is a revenue-based, areawide policy that may be purchased as a stand-alone policy or purchased in addition to any other individual or area policy. Indemnifies losses in county revenue of greater than 10% of expected revenue but not more than the deductible level (e.g., 25%) selected by the producer for the underlying individual policy (or not more than 30% used as stand-alone policy). Coverage is based on the expected price used for existing area-wide policies and the higher of expected county yields established for existing area-wide policies or the 5-year Olympic average county yield (Olympic average excludes the high and low years), using data from USDA's Risk Management Agency and/or National Agricultural Statistics Service or other data as considered appropriate by the Secretary). Indemnities are paid based on the amount that the actual county revenue falls

Previous Law/Policy	2014 Farm Bill (P.L. 113-79)
	short of the expected county revenue, as applied to the individual coverage of the producer. For individual producers, indemnities for STAX and other policies cannot overlap. The premium subsidy is 80% plus the amount for A&O. The calculated premium covers: (1) anticipated losses and a reasonable reserve, and (2) an amount for administrative and operating expenses. Policies are to be offered in all producing counties at the county level, or on the basis of a larger geographic area if necessary. Separate coverage levels are available for irrigated and nonirrigated practices. A factor of not more than 120% is available to increase protection per acre *[Sec. 11017]* Cotton is not a covered commodity eligible for Price Loss Coverage (PLC) or Agriculture Risk Coverage (ARC) in Title I of the 2014 farm bill. *[Sec. 1111(6)]*
No comparable provision.	Beginning with the 2015 crop year, the FCIC shall make available a revenue policy for peanut producers and use the Rotterdam price index or other appropriate prices as determined by the Secretary. The effective price may be adjusted to correct distortions, but the adjustment must be done in an open and transparent manner and a report must be submitted to Congress describing the reasons for the adjustment. *[Sec. 11018] The* approval of a peanut revenue policy is to be made a priority for FCIC. *[Sec. 11010(a)]*
Correcting Errors	
To improve program compliance and integrity, FCIC shall work with approved insurance providers to address program compliance and integrity issues. *[7 U.S.C. 1515(a)(2)]* Inaccurate information on an insurance application can result in noncompliance, which voids the policy and may result in civil fines and program disqualification for up to 5 years. *[7 U.S.C.*	FCIC shall establish procedures that allow an agent and approved insurance provider to correct (within a reasonable amount of time) errors in information that is provided by a producer to ensure that the eligibility (and other) information is correct and consistent with information reported by the producer for other USDA programs. Additional provisions allow for corrections of data

Table A-1. (Continued)

Previous Law/Policy	2014 Farm Bill (P.L. 113-79)
1515(h)] The FCIC and USDA's Farm Service Agency shall reconcile producer-derived information on at least an annual basis in order to identify and address any discrepancies. *[7 U.S.C. 1515(c)]*	issued by the Farm Service Agency or electronic transmission errors made by an agent, approved insurance provider, or USDA agencies. Correction may only be made if they do not allow the producer to: (1) avoid ineligibility requirements for insurance or obtain a disproportionate benefit; (2) obtain and enhance an insurance guarantee or indemnity if a cause of loss exists or has occurred before any correction has been made, or avoid premium owed if no loss is likely to occur; or (3) avoid an obligation or requirement under any federal or state law. Any corrections made within a reasonable amount of time shall not be subject to late filing fees. Also, provides authority to allow a producer to purchase crop insurance after the sales closing date under certain conditions. *[Sec. 11019]*
Implementation and Fraud Detection	
USDA is to ensure that new hardware and software for administering the program are compatible with that already used by USDA agencies in order to maximize data sharing needed for proper program delivery. *[7 U.S.C. 1515(j)]* Funding is provided from the insurance fund: $15 million for each of FY2008 through FY2010 and not more than $9 million in FY2011. *[7 U.S.C. 1515(k]*	USDA shall develop and implement an Acreage Crop Reporting Streamlining Initiative (ACRSI) project to allow producers to report acreage and other information directly to USDA. FCIC may use up to $14 million in FY2014 and $9 million per year for FY2015 through FY2018 from the insurance fund. An additional $5 million per year is available for each of FY2015-2018 if the ACRSI project is substantially completed by September 30, 2015. USDA shall notify Congress on the status of the project no later than July 1, 2015. *[Sec. 11020]*
FCIC may use up to $3.5 million of the insurance fund to pay for costs associated with implementing plans of insurance and for review of policies. *[7 U.S.C. 1516(b)(2)]*	Adds authority to use up to $9 million per year of the insurance fund to pay for costs associated with maintaining program integrity and compliance activities and to assist in maintaining program actuarial soundness and financial integrity. *[Sec. 11021]*
Research and Development Priorities	

Previous Law/Policy	2014 Farm Bill (P.L. 113-79)
FCIC may enter into contracts to carry out research and development for new crop insurance policies but may not conduct research itself. FCIC shall establish as one of the highest research priorities the development of a pasture, range, and forage program. *[7 U.S.C. 1522(c)]*	In addition to contracting, allows FCIC to conduct research and development activities to maintain or improve existing policies or develop new policies. *[Sec. 11022(a)(1-3)]* Replaces the priority on pasture, range, and forage program with policies that increase participation by producers of underserved agricultural commodities, including sweet sorghum, biomass sorghum, rice, peanuts, sugarcane, alfalfa, pennycress, dedicated energy crops, and specialty crops. *[Sec. 11022(a)(5)]* Requires FCIC to enter into contracts to conduct research and development on policies for: (1) the margin between the market value of catfish and input costs; (2) biomass sorghum and sweet sorghum grown expressly for the purpose of producing a feedstock for renewable biofuel, renewable electricity, or biobased products; (3) whole farm insurance (see below); (4) poultry business interruptions insurance for poultry growers, including losses due to bankruptcy of an integrator (ownerprocessor), with research contract entered within 180 days of enactment of the farm bill and a summary report submitted to Congress within 1 year of enactment; and (5) alfalfa crop insurance, with a summary report submitted to Congress within 1 year of enactment of the farm bill. *[Sec. 11022(a)(7)]* Requires FCIC to contract for studies on: (1) insuring swine producers for a catastrophic event, (2) insuring poultry producers for a catastrophic event, (3) providing production or revenue loss coverage for specialty crops related to food safety and contaminations issues, including public announcements. FCIC must submit reports on each to Congress within 1 year of enactment of the farm bill. *[Sec. 11022(a)(7)]*
Adjusted Gross Revenue (AGR) and AGR-Lite policies insure revenue of the entire farm rather than an individual crop. Both use	Unless FCIC approves an enhanced whole farm insurance plan by 2016, FCIC shall conduct activities or enter into contracts to

Table A-1. (Continued)

Previous Law/Policy	2014 Farm Bill (P.L. 113-79)
a producer's five-year historical farm average revenue as reported on the Internal Revenue Service (IRS) tax return form (Schedule F or equivalent forms). Coverage levels range from 65% to 80% of historical revenue, and maximum liability is $6.5 million for AGR and $1million for AGR-Lite. *[7 U.S.C. 1523]*	carry out research and development to develop an enhanced version of the whole farm risk management insurance plan. Available coverage is increased from 80% to 85%, and maximum liability is $1.5 million (up from $1 million for AGR-Lite). Eligible producers include direct-toconsumer marketers and producers who produce multiple agricultural commodities, including specialty crops, industrial crops, livestock, and aquaculture products. The FCIC may provide diversification-based additional coverage payment rates, premium discounts, or other enhanced benefits in recognition of the risk management benefits of crop and livestock diversification strategies for producers. The FCIC also may include coverage for the value of any packing, packaging, or any other similar on-farm activity that FCIC determines to be the minimum required in order to remove the commodity from the field. *[Sec. 11022(a)(7)]*
Miscellaneous	
Organic policies: Requires FCIC to improve coverage for organic crops. *[U.S.C. 1522(c)(10)]* As of early 2014, USDA offered organic price elections for 16 crops, which increases the insurable value for organic producers.	By 2015, requires FCIC to offer price elections that reflect actual retail or wholesale prices of organic (not conventional) crops. Applies to all organic crops produced in compliance with standards issued by USDA under the Organic Foods Production Act of 1990. FCIC must submit an annual report to Congress on crop insurance for organic crops. *[Sec. 11023]*
Partnerships for risk management development and implementation: FCIC is authorized to enter into partnerships with public and private entities for the purpose of increasing the availability of loss mitigation, financial, and other risk management tools for producers, with a priority given to risk management tools for	Revises the purpose and objective of partnerships to also include improving analysis tools and technology regarding compliance or identifying and using innovative compliance strategies. *[Sec. 11024]* Adds "farm financial benchmarking" to the list of partnership objectives. The term is

Previous Law/Policy	2014 Farm Bill (P.L. 113-79)
producers of agricultural commodities covered by the noninsured crop assistance program (NAP), specialty crops, and underserved agricultural commodities. *[U.S.C. 1522(d)]*	defined as the process of comparing the performance of an agricultural enterprise against the performance of other similar enterprises through the use of comparable and reliable data, in order to identify business management strengths, weaknesses, and steps necessary to improve business profitability. *[Sec. 11027]*
Pilot programs: FCIC may conduct a pilot program submitted to and approved by the Board to evaluate whether a proposal or new risk management tool is suitable for the marketplace and addresses the needs of producers. After the completion of pilot program, FCIC shall submit to Congress a report on its operation and include recommendations on implementing the program on a national basis. *[7 U.S.C. 1523(a)]* FCIC shall not conduct any pilot program that provides insurance protection against a risk if a policy is generally available from private companies. *[7 U.S.C. 1523(a)(2)]*	Eliminates the requirement that FCIC evaluate pilot programs and submit a report to Congress. *[Sec. 11025]* FCIC is authorized to conduct two or more pilot programs to provide producers of underserved specialty crops and livestock commodities (including pasture, rangeland, and forage) with index-based weather insurance. The FCIC Board shall approve two or more proposed policies, if certain conditions are met, including experience and financial requirements of the approved provider. Priority is given to new kinds of coverage for specialty crops and livestock that previously had no available crop insurance or have low participation under existing coverage. The subsidy shall not exceed 60% of the estimated premium amount. Administrative and operating expenses are to be reimbursed, but federal reinsurance, research and development costs, and other reimbursements or maintenance fees are not provided for these policies. Policies may be sold only by the approved provider that submits the application; others may also sell them if maintenance fees are paid to the provider who submitted the proposal. The FCIC must develop and publish procedures that (1) require each approved insurance provider to report sales, acreage, and claim data to allow FCIC to evaluate sales and performance; and (2) ensure that the products do not have a significant adverse impact on the crop insurance delivery system, are in the best interests of producers, and do not result in a

Table A-1. (Continued)

Previous Law/Policy	2014 Farm Bill (P.L. 113-79)
	reduction of program integrity. Policies cannot be substantially similar to privately available hail insurance. Mandatory funding from FCIC fund is limited to $12.5 million per year for FY2015-2018. *[Sec. 11026]*
Education and risk management assistance: The Secretary, acting through the National Institute of Food and Agriculture, shall establish a program under which competitive grants are made to qualified public and private entities (including land grant colleges, cooperative extension services, and colleges or universities) for the purpose of educating agricultural producers about the full range of risk management activities, including futures, options, agricultural trade options, crop insurance, cash forward contracting, debt reduction, production diversification, farm resources risk reduction, and other risk management strategies. *[7 U.S.C. 1524(a)(3)(A)]*	Adds farm financial benchmarking to the list of risk management activities. *[Sec. 11027]*
No comparable provision.	Various technical amendments, including a provision that requires notice to Congress if the Standard Reinsurance Agreement is renegotiated. *[Sec. 11028]*
Noninsured Crop Disaster Assistance Program (NAP)	
The Noninsured Crop Disaster Assistance Program (NAP) has permanent authority under Section 196 of the Federal Agriculture Improvement and Reform Act of 1996, and receives such sums as necessary in mandatory funding. Growers of crops not insurable under the crop insurance program are eligible for NAP. A payment is made to an eligible producer whose actual production is less than 50% of the established (historical) yield for the crop. The payment rate is 55% of the average market price. Producers pay a fee of $250 per crop per county, or $750 per producer per county, not	In Title XII—Miscellaneous: Makes available for crop years 2015-2018 additional coverage under NAP at 50% to 65% of established yield and 100% of average market price. Premium for additional coverage is 5.25% times the product of the selected coverage level and value of production (acreage times yield times average market price). The maximum premium is 5.25% times the payment limit ($125,000). Extends fee waiver for basic NAP coverage to beginning and socially disadvantaged farmers. Premium for additional NAP

Previous Law/Policy	2014 Farm Bill (P.L. 113-79)
to exceed $1,875 per producer. The fee is waived for a limited resource farmer. The Farm Service Agency administers the program. *[7 USC 7333]*	coverage is reduced by 50% for limited resource, beginning, and socially disadvantaged farmers. For producers with fruit crop losses in 2012, payments associated with additional coverage are made retroactively (minus premium fees) in counties declared a disaster due to freeze or frost. Maintains industrial crops as eligible for NAP but specifies that industrial crops include those grown expressly for the purpose of producing a feedstock for renewable biofuel, renewable electricity, or biobased products. Specifically adds sweet sorghum and biomass sorghum to list of eligible crops for NAP. Crops and grasses for grazing are not eligible for additional coverage but remain eligible for catastrophic coverage. *[Sec. 12305(a)]*
The total amount of payments received per person for any crop year may not exceed $100,000. *[7 USC 7333(i)(2)]*	Payment limit is increased to $125,000. *[Sec. 12305(a)(2)]*

Source: CRS.

End Notes

[1] Additional background on the federal crop insurance program is available in CRS Report R40532, Federal Crop Insurance: Background.

[2] Randall A. Kramer, "Federal Crop Insurance 1938-1982," Agricultural History, vol. 57, no. 2 (April 1983), pp. 181- 200.

[3] An example of hail or fire insurance is https://www.rainhail.com/pdf_files/MKTG/MKTG_4000.pdf. Examples of other single peril coverage include (1) insurance for specific weather variables such as low temperature offered by Total Weather Insurance, http://climate.com/products/total-weather-insurance/; and (2) riders on federal policies to increase crop price protection contained in the Hudson Insurance Price Flex contract, http://www.hudsoncrop.com/index.php?option=com_content&view=article&id=51&Itemid=70.

[4] Vincent H. Smith and Barry K. Goodwin, "Private and Public Roles in Providing Agricultural Insurance in the United States," in Public Insurance and Private Markets, ed. Jeffrey R. Brown (Washington, DC: AEI Press, 2010), p. 184.

[5] Joseph W. Glauber, "Crop Insurance Reconsidered," Amer. J. Agr. Econ., vol. 86, no. 5 (2004), pp. 1179-1195.

[6] Producers who grow a crop not covered by crop insurance can purchase coverage through the Noninsured Crop Disaster Assistance Program (NAP). For more information, see CRS Report RS21212, Agricultural Disaster Assistance.

[7] This transfer of risk is accomplished through a set of reinsurance funds maintained by FCIC. The assigned risk fund, for example, is used by companies for policies believed to be high-risk because it provides the most loss protection to insurance companies through "stop-loss" coverage that reinsures against state-level disasters.

[8] As part of the transition, farm payments are made for upland cotton for the 2014 crop year, and for 2015 if STAX is not available. Payment acres in 2014 equal 60% of 2013 cotton base acres and 36.5% of 2013 cotton base acres in 2015. For more information on PLC and ARC, see CRS Report R43448, Farm Commodity Provisions in the 2014 Farm Bill (P.L. 113-79). For information on the cotton trade case, see CRS Report R43336, Status of the WTO BrazilU.S. Cotton Case.

[9] The revenue guarantee is the producer's selected coverage level times the expected per-acre revenue prior to planting (expected yield times expected price). The expected county yield is the higher of either the historical yield used for existing area-wide policies or the five-year county area average yield, excluding the high and low years, using data from USDA's Risk Management Agency and/or National Agricultural Statistics Service. As with many crop insurance policies for major crops, the expected price component of the guarantee for STAX is based on the average futures market price for cotton prior to planting time. In a previous farm bill proposal in 2012, specifically the 2012 House Agriculture Committee bill (H.R. 6083), a minimum price of $0.6861 per pound would have been used in the calculation of the insurance guarantee if it was higher than the expected market price. Inclusion of a minimum guarantee price would have provided enhanced the price protection for producers but would have introduced price supports into crop insurance and complicated the expected resolution of the cotton trade case.

[10] For numerical examples of SCO, see Nick Paulson, University of Illinois, Understanding the Supplemental Coverage Option (SCO) in the 2014 Farm Bill, March 12, 2014, http://www.farmdoc.illinois.edu/webinars/downloads/PDF/ 120314_farm_bill_sco_paulson.pdf.

[11] The two approaches differ in that ARC price guarantee is based on historical market prices while the crop insurance guarantees (including SCO) is based on expected market prices prior to planting. For more, see CRS Report R43448, Farm Commodity Provisions in the 2014 Farm Bill (P.L. 113-79).

[12] U.S. Department of Agriculture, FSA-RMA Farm Bill Listening Session, Washington, DC, March 27, 2014.

[13] AGR-Lite has maximum liability of $1 million compared with $6.5 million for AGR. AGR-Lite does not limit the share of livestock revenue in the guarantee (limited to 35% in AGR). Both products use a producer's five-year historical farm average revenue as reported on the Internal Revenue Service (IRS) tax return form (Schedule F or equivalent forms). Coverage levels range from 65% to 80% of historical revenue.

[14] USDA defines a limited resource farmer or rancher as one who has farm sales not more than $172,800 and household income at or below the national poverty level for a family of four. "Socially disadvantaged" means a group whose members have been subjected to racial or ethnic prejudice because of their identity as members of a group without regard to their individual qualities. (7 U.S.C. 2279(e)).

[15] In the House farm bill debate, prior to the floor vote on the farm bill on June 20, 2013 (which was rejected by a vote of 195-234), the House rejected H.Amdt. 216 by a vote of 208-217.

It would have limited premium subsidies to those producers with an adjusted gross income under $250,000, limited per-person premium subsidies to $50,000, and capped crop insurance providers' reimbursement of administrative and operating expenses at $900 million and reduced their rate of return to 12%.

In: The Farm Safety Net: Key Components ISBN: 978-1-63463-731-2
Editor: Jodie R. Haggard

Chapter 2

FARM COMMODITY PROVISIONS IN THE 2014 FARM BILL (P.L. 113-79)*

Dennis A. Shields

SUMMARY

The farm commodity program provisions in Title I of the Agricultural Act of 2014 (P.L. 113-79, the 2014 farm bill) include three types of support for crop years 2014-2018:

- *Price Loss Coverage (PLC) payments,* which are triggered when the national average farm price for a covered commodity (e.g., wheat, corn, soybeans, rice, and peanuts) is below its statutorily fixed "reference price";
- *Agriculture Risk Coverage (ARC) payments,* as an alternative to PLC, which are triggered when crop revenue is below its guaranteed level based on a multiyear moving average of historical crop revenue; and
- *Marketing Assistance Loans (MALs),* which offer interim financing for the loan commodities (covered crops plus several others) and, if prices fall below loan rates set in statute, additional low-price protection, sometimes paid as *loan deficiency payments (LDPs).*

---

* This is an edited, reformatted and augmented version of a Congressional Research Service publication R43448, prepared for Members and Committees of Congress, dated March 28, 2014.

The enacted 2014 farm bill eliminated "direct payments," which were provided annually to producers and landowners of covered commodities from 1996 to 2013 based on historical production and a fixed payment rate set in statute. All farm program support now consists of variable payments. The PLC and ARC programs are enhanced relative to their predecessors via higher reference prices for PLC and more "local" coverage for ARC (whereby payments are triggered by county or individual losses rather than at the state level). In a major departure from previous farm bills and in response to a trade dispute with Brazil, upland cotton is no longer a covered commodity, with support for that crop now provided by a new crop insurance policy called the Stacked Income Protection Plan (STAX).

Approximately three-fourths of the 10-year, $47 billion in savings associated with the elimination of 2008 farm bill commodity programs was used to offset the costs of revising the overall farm safety net, specifically farm programs in Title I of the 2014 farm bill, adding permanent disaster assistance (also in Title I), enhancing the permanently authorized federal crop insurance program (Title XI), and enhancing the Noninsured Crop Disaster Assistance Program or NAP (Title XII). Crop insurance is available for more than 100 crops, including fruits and vegetables, and is designed primarily to cover losses from natural disasters. Farm programs do not require a participation fee, while crop insurance requires participating farmers to pay part of program costs.

The enacted 2014 farm bill sets a $125,000 per person cap on the total of PLC, ARC, marketing loan gains and loan deficiency payments. The limit applies to the total from all covered commodities except peanuts, which has a separate $125,000 limit. Also, to be eligible for payments, persons must be "actively engaged" in farming. The 2014 farm bill instructs USDA to write regulations (beginning with the 2015 crop year) that define "significant contribution of active personal management" to more clearly and objectively implement existing law. A single, total adjusted gross income (AGI) limit for payment eligibility is established at $900,000, which is less than the sum of the two separate limits (farm and non-farm) in the 2008 farm bill.

The Congressional Budget Office cost estimate (score) of the Title I provisions represents five-year savings of $6.3 billion and 10-year savings of $14.3 billion (both relative to baseline projections made in May 2013 assuming continuation of the 2008 farm bill). If these scores are added to the 2013 CBO baseline of budget outlays used to write the farm bill, then CBO's estimated cost of Title I is $23.6 billion for FY2014-2018 and $44.5 billion over 10 years.

INTRODUCTION

On February 7, 2014, President Obama signed into law a new five-year omnibus farm bill, the Agricultural Act of 2014 (H.R. 2642; P.L. 113-79, the 2014 farm bill). The House had voted, 251- 166, to approve the conference report (H.Rept. 113-333) on January 29, 2014, and the Senate approved the conference report on February 4, 2014, by a vote of 68-32. The U.S. Department of Agriculture (USDA) is now implementing the provisions, most of which take effect this year.

This report describes the farm commodity programs in Title I of the 2014 farm bill for "covered commodities" such as wheat, corn, soybeans, rice, and peanuts. Producer support is provided for the 2014-2018 crop years primarily through either statutory ("reference") prices or historical revenue guarantees based on the five most recent years of crop prices and yields.[1]

Important policy developments in the new law are also discussed and compared to prior law. The most significant policy change for commodity programs in the 2014 farm bill was the elimination of fixed direct payments and the enhancement of variable payments to farmers and landowners when crop prices or revenue declines.

Table A-1 provides detailed descriptions of farm commodity program provisions compared with prior law.

BACKGROUND

Policy Rationale for Farm Subsidies

Federal farm support began in the 1930s through Depression-era efforts to raise farm household income when commodity prices were low because of prolonged weak consumer demand. While initially intended to be a temporary effort, the commodity support programs survived, but have been modified away from supply control and management of commodity stocks (which was designed to prop up prices) into direct income support payments. The 2014 farm bill continues traditional farm support via variable payments relative to statutory price levels or historical crop revenue.

Proponents of farm commodity programs argue that federal involvement in the sector is needed to stabilize and support farm incomes by shifting some of the risks to the federal government. These risks include short-term market price instability and longer-term capacity adjustments. Proponents see the goal of farm policy as maintaining the economic health of the nation's farm sector so that it can use its comparative advantage in feeding the nation and competing in the global market for food and fiber. Critics argue that farm commodity programs waste taxpayer dollars, distort production of certain crops, capitalize benefits to the owners of the resources, encourage concentration of production, and comparatively harm smaller domestic producers and farmers in lower-income foreign nations.

Authorizing Legislation

The authority for USDA to operate farm commodity programs comes from three permanent laws, as amended: the Agricultural Adjustment Act of 1938 (P.L. 75-430), the Agricultural Act of 1949 (P.L. 81-439), and the Commodity Credit Corporation (CCC) Charter Act of 1948 (P.L. 80-806). Congress typically alters these laws through multi-year omnibus farm bills to address current market conditions, budget constraints, or other concerns.

If a new farm bill is not enacted when an old one expires, farm programs would revert to the permanent laws mentioned above for most of the major program crops. Under permanent law, eligible commodities would be supported at levels much higher than they are now, and many of the currently supported commodities might not be eligible. Since reverting to permanent law is incompatible with current national economic objectives, global trading rules, and federal budgetary policies, pressure builds at the end of one farm bill to enact another.[2]

The 2014 farm bill (P.L. 113-79) contains the most recent version of the farm commodity support programs. It supersedes the commodity provisions of previous farm bills, and suspends the relevant price support provisions of permanent law.

Eligible Commodities

Federal support exists for about two dozen farm commodities representing about one-third of gross farm sales. During FY2005-FY2014, five crops (corn, cotton, wheat, rice, and soybeans) accounted for about 90% of these payments.[3]

- Under the 2014 farm bill, the "covered commodities" are the primary crops eligible for farm support: wheat, oats, and barley (including wheat, oats, and barley used for haying and grazing); corn, grain sorghum, long grain rice, medium grain rice, and pulse crops (dry peas, lentils, small chickpeas, and large chickpeas); soybeans, other oilseeds (including sunflower seed, rapeseed, canola, safflower, flaxseed, mustard seed, crambe, and sesame seed), and peanuts.
- In a major departure from all previous farm bills and in response to a trade dispute with Brazil, upland cotton is no longer a covered crop, with support for that crop now provided by a new crop insurance policy called the Stacked Income Protection Plan (STAX).[4]
- "Loan commodities" include all of the "covered commodities" plus upland cotton, extra long staple cotton, wool, mohair, and honey. These commodities are eligible for the marketing loan program only.
- The 2014 farm bill replaces the dairy product price support program and Milk Income Loss Contract (MILC) payments with new dairy programs to (1) protect producer margins (milk prices minus feed costs), and (2) buy excess dairy products to boost demand when margins drop below certain levels.
- Sugar support is indirect through import quotas, price guarantees, and domestic marketing allotments. No direct payments are made to growers and processors. There was no change to the sugar program in the 2014 farm bill.

Meats, poultry, fruits, vegetables, nuts, hay, and nursery products (about two-thirds of farm sales) do not receive direct support or payments under the commodity programs of the farm bill. However, livestock and tree fruit producers receive disaster support under Title I of the 2014 farm bill. (See *Table A-1* and CRS Report, *Agricultural Disaster Assistance*, for a description of disaster programs.) Also, under the permanently authorized federal crop insurance program, subsidized crop insurance is available for more than 100 crops, including fruits and vegetables which are not supported by farm programs. Crop insurance is designed primarily to cover losses from natural disasters and within-season price or revenue declines.

Definition of "Farm"

The definition of "farm" used to administer the commodity programs is different from other statistical or perceived definitions of farms. Under Farm Service Agency (FSA) regulations, a "farm" for program payment purposes is one or more tracts of land considered to be a separate operation.[5] Land in a farm does not need to be contiguous; however, all tracts within a farm must have the same operator and the same owner (unless all owners agree to combine multiple tracts into a single FSA farm). Thus, one producer may be operating several "farms" if he/she is renting land from several landlords, or has purchased land in several tracts.

Base Acres

For the purpose of calculating program payments, the term "base acres" is the historical planted acreage on each FSA farm, using a multi-year average from as far back as the 1980s.[6] Technically, a farm's base with respect to a covered commodity is the number of acres in effect under the 2008 farm bill (7 U.S.C. 8702, 8751) as of September 30, 2013, subject to any reallocation, adjustment, or reduction under the 2014 farm bill. Base is calculated for each covered commodity and transfers to the new owner when land is sold, making the new landowner eligible for farm programs.

Because a farmer's actual plantings may differ from farm base acres, program payments may not necessarily align with financial losses associated with market prices or crop revenue. In order to better match program payments with farm risk, the 2014 farm bill provides farmers with a onetime opportunity to update individual crop base acres by reallocating acreage within their current base to match their actual crop mix (plantings) during 2009-2012. Farmers can also choose to not reallocate their base if they expect payments to be maximized under their current base. In the case of cotton, which is no longer a covered commodity, former cotton base acres are renamed "generic base" and added to a producer's base for potential payments if a covered crop is planted on the farm.[7]

"Partially Decoupled" Payments

Payments under the new programs in the 2014 farm bill are made on base acres, not current plantings.[8] This feature—decoupling payments from current plantings—is intended to better comply with World Trade Organization (WTO) rules on domestic support and to minimize any influence on producer behavior and prevent any subsequent market distortion. The payments are considered "partially decoupled" because the payment amount remains connected to current market prices. In the 2008 farm bill, farm payments were calculated using either base or planted area, depending upon the program.

Eligible Producers

The 2014 farm bill defines a producer (for purposes of farm program benefits) as an owner-operator, landlord, tenant, or sharecropper that shares in the risk of producing a crop and is entitled to a share of the crop produced on the farm. For payment eligibility, a term commonly used in federal regulations is "actively engaged in farming," which generally means providing significant contributions of capital (land or equipment) and labor and/or management, and receiving a share of the crop as compensation. The 2014 farm bill requires USDA to write new regulations that define "significant contribution of active personal management." See "Payment Limits," below.

Producers do not pay to participate in farm programs. However, an individual must comply with certain conservation and planting flexibility rules. Conservation rules include protecting wetlands, preventing erosion, and controlling weeds. Planting flexibility rules allow crops other than the program crop to be grown, but under the 2014 farm bill, eligible payment acreage is reduced when fruits, vegetables, or wild rice are planted in excess of 15% of base acres (or 35% depending upon a farmer's program choice discussed below). Also, a producer on a farm may not receive farm program payments if the sum of the base acres on the farm is 10 acres or less.

A farm enterprise usually involves some combination of owned and rented land. Two types of rental arrangements are common: cash rent and share rent. Under cash rental contracts, the tenant pays a fixed cash rent to the landlord. The landlord receives the same rent, bears no risk in production, and thus is not eligible to receive program payments. The tenant bears all of the risk, takes all of the harvest, and receives all of the government subsidy.

Under share rental contracts, the tenant usually supplies most or all of the labor and machinery, while the landlord supplies land and perhaps some machinery or management. Both the landlord and the tenant bear risk in producing a crop and receive a portion of the harvest.[9] Both are eligible to share in the government subsidy.

Even though tenants might receive all of the government payments under cash rent arrangements, they might not keep all of the benefits if landlords demand higher rent. Economists widely agree that a large portion of government farm payments passes through to landlords, since government payments boost the rental value of land. The amount of total land in farms rented by farm operators has ranged between 34% and 43% of farmland during 1964-2007.[10]

Eliminated 2008 Farm Bill Programs

Under the enacted 2014 farm bill (P.L. 113-79), farm support for traditional program crops is restructured by eliminating the direct payment (DP) and counter-cyclical payment (CCP) programs, and the Average Crop Revenue Election (ACRE) program. For the 1996 through 2013 crop years, direct payments were made to producers and landowners based on historical production of corn, wheat, soybeans, cotton, rice, peanuts, and other "covered" crops. Direct payments lost political support in recent years because recipients did not need to suffer an income loss in order to receive a payment. Approximately three-fourths of the 10-year, $47 billion in savings associated with the elimination of current farm programs was used to offset the costs of revising farm programs in Title I of the 2014 farm bill, adding permanent disaster assistance (also in Title I), enhancing the permanently-authorized federal crop insurance program (Title XI), and enhancing the Noninsured Crop Disaster Assistance Program or NAP (Title XII).

Farm Commodity Program Provisions

The farm commodity program provisions in Title I of the 2014 farm bill include three types of support for crop years 2014-2018:

- *Price Loss Coverage (PLC) payments,* which are triggered when the national average farm price for a covered commodity is below its statutorily-fixed "reference price";
- *Agriculture Risk Coverage (ARC) payments,* as an alternative to PLC, which are triggered when crop revenue is below its guaranteed level based on a multiyear moving average of historical crop revenue; and
- *Marketing Assistance Loans (MALs)* that offer interim financing for the loan commodities (covered crops plus several others as indicated above) and, if prices fall below loan rates set in statute, additional low-price protection, sometimes paid as *loan deficiency payments (LDPs).*

Farmers with base acres of covered commodities have a one-time irrevocable decision to choose between PLC and "county" ARC (based on a county guarantee) on a commodity-by-commodity basis for each farm. Alternatively, all covered crops on a farm can be enrolled in "individual" ARC, which is based on a farm-level guarantee. (See "Agriculture Risk Coverage (ARC)," below.) If no choice is made, the producer forfeits any payments for the 2014 crop year and the farm is enrolled automatically in PLC for the 2015-2018 crop years. The "optimal" decision depends in part on expected prices through 2018 relative to guarantees in each program.

The PLC and ARC programs are similar conceptually to the 2008 farm bill's counter-cyclical payment (CCP) program and Average Crop Revenue Election (ACRE) program, respectively. However, compared with the previous programs, they have enhanced levels of protection from low prices (i.e., higher price parameters in PLC) or revenue loss (i.e., county- or farm-level guarantees for ARC rather than state-level in ACRE).

PLC and ARC payments are proportional to base acres, and not planted acres.[11] Payments are made with a lag of approximately one year as annual price and yield data are compiled for USDA's calculations. USDA is to issue payments beginning October 1 after the end of each marketing year, which varies by crop. For example, the marketing year for corn harvested in fall of 2014 ends in August 2015.

Marketing assistance loans are available for covered crops and other loan commodities. The program continues mostly unchanged from the 2008 farm bill, with loan rates set at relatively low levels compared to historical prices.

All three types of payments are subject to a combined payment limit of $125,000 per person. Also, the income limit for program eligibility is

$900,000 for adjusted gross income (three-year average). See "Payment Limits" and "Adjusted Gross Income (AGI) Limit," below.

Price Loss Coverage (PLC)

For each covered commodity on a farm, producers may select the Price Loss Coverage (PLC) program to receive a payment on 85% of base acres when the annual national average farm price is below the reference price set in statute. This option could be attractive if farmers expect farm prices to drop below statutory minimums.

Payments are proportional to a farm's base acres, historical farm yield, and the difference between the reference price and the annual farm price. Hence payments are generally "decoupled" from planted acreage and actual yield but not price. PLC payments operate the same as CCPs under the 2008 farm bill, which have been reported to the WTO by the United States as "amber box" subsidies, and thus limited in size together with other amber box subsidies.

Commodity groups successfully argued for an increase in reference prices relative to the payment trigger levels in the 2008 farm bill (i.e., target price minus direct payment rate). For example, the payment trigger level has been raised by 51% for wheat, 57% for corn, 51% for soybeans, 72% for rice (98% for temperate Japonica rice), and 17% for peanuts. Reference prices and a comparison with 2008 farm bill parameters for each covered commodity are shown in *Table 1.*

The PLC payment formula is 85% *times* the number of base acres *times* historical payment yield *times* the difference between the reference price and the annual farm price (or loan rate if higher). See *Figure 1* for a graphical interpretation of the formula and *Figure 2* for a hypothetical example for rice. The historical payment yield is equal to 90% of the 2008-2012 average yield per planted acre for the farm. As an alternative, the producer can keep the program yield used for calculating CCPs in the 2008 farm bill (generally based on 1998-2001 yields).

Agriculture Risk Coverage (ARC)

Producers more concerned about declines in crop revenue (i.e., yield times price) than just price can select the county Agriculture Risk Coverage (ARC) program as an alternative to PLC for each covered commodity. Payments are made on 85% of base acres when annual crop revenue is less than 86% of its historical level.

If farmers prefer individual farm level protection, they must enroll *all* covered crops on the farm in the ARC-individual coverage option instead of selecting between PLC and county ARC for each crop.

Table 1. Loan Rates and Reference Prices in the 2014 Farm Bill

	2008 and 2014 farm bills	*Price at which a payment is triggered:*		
		2008 farm bill	*2014 farm bill*	
	Loan Rate	*Target Price minus Direct Payment Rate*	*Reference Price*	*% change from 2008 farm bill*
Wheat, $/bu	2.94	4.17 – 0.52 = *3.65*	5.50	+51%
Corn, $/bu	1.95	2.63 – 0.28 = *2.35*	3.70	+57%
Sorghum, $/bu	1.95	2.63 – 0.35 = *2.28*	3.95	+73%
Barley, $/bu	1.95	2.63 – 0.24 = *2.39*	4.95	+107%
Oats, $/bu	1.39	1.79 – 0.024 = *1.766*	2.40	+36%
Upland Cotton, $/lb	2008 farm bill: 0.52	0.7125 – 0.0667 = *0.6458*	n.a.	n.a.
	2014 farm bill: 0.45 to 0.52			
ELS cotton, $/lb	0.7977	n.a.	n.a.	n.a.
Rice, $/cwt	6.50	10.50 – 2.35 = *8.15*	14.00; 16.10 for temperate japonica	+72%; +98% for temperate japonica
Soybeans, $/bu	5.00	6 – 0.44 = *5.56*	8.40	+51%
Minor oilseeds, $/lb	0.1009	0.1268 – 0.008 = *0.1188*	0.2015	+70%
Peanuts, $/ton	355	495-36 = *459*	535	+17%
Peas, dry, $/cwt	5.40	8.32 – 0 = *8.32*	11.00	+32%
Lentils, $/cwt	11.28	12.81 – 0 = *12.81*	19.97	+56%
Sm.chickpeas, $/cwt	7.43	10.36 – 0 = *10.36*	19.04	+84%
Lg.chickpeas, $/cwt	11.28	12.81 – 0 = *12.81*	21.54	+68%
Wool, graded, $/lb	1.15	n.a.	n.a.	n.a.
Wool, nongraded	0.40	n.a.	n.a.	n.a.
Mohair $/lb	4.20	n.a.	n.a.	n.a.
Honey, $/lb	0.69	n.a.	n.a.	n.a.
Sugar, raw cane, $/lb	0.1875	n.a.	n.a.	n.a.
Sugar, beet, $/lb	0.2409	n.a.	n.a.	n.a.

Source: CRS.

Note: n.a. = not applicable.

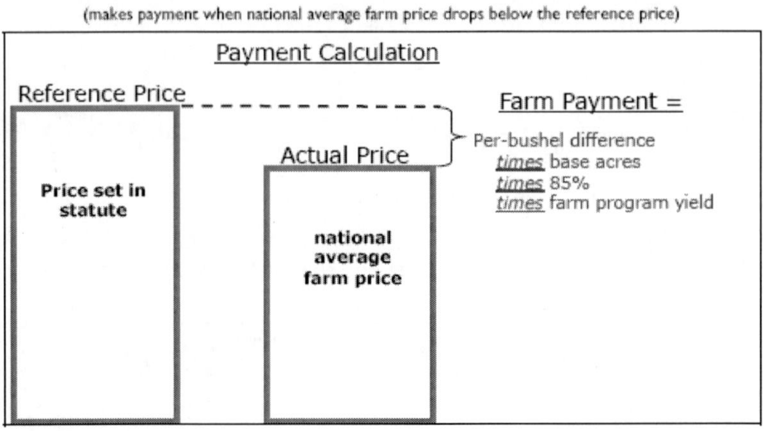

Source: CRS.

Note: In a declining market, the per-bushel payment rate increases until the farm price drops below the loan rate. At this point, benefits under the Marketing Assistance Loan Program may become available.

Figure 1. Price Loss Coverage (PLC).

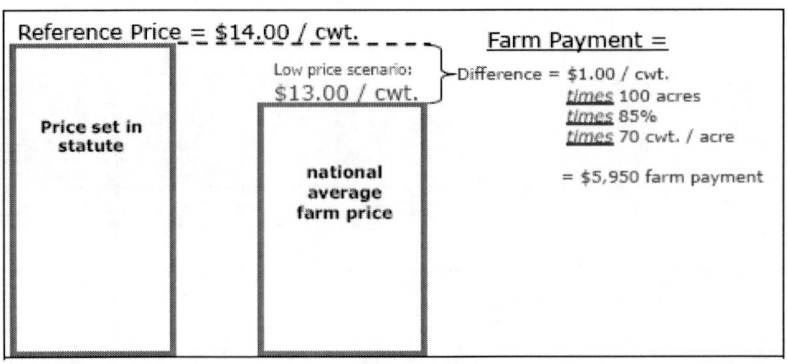

Source: CRS.

Notes: In a declining market, the per-bushel payment rate increases until the farm price drops below the loan rate ($6.50/cwt. for rice). If market prices decline further, benefits under the Marketing Assistance Loan Program may become available.

Figure 2. Price Loss Coverage (PLC): Low Price Scenario for Rice.

Agriculture Risk Coverage (ARC)

Producers more concerned about declines in crop revenue (i.e., yield times price) than just price can select the county Agriculture Risk Coverage (ARC) program as an alternative to PLC for each covered commodity. Payments are made on 85% of base acres when annual crop revenue is less than 86% of its historical level.

If farmers prefer individual farm level protection, they must enroll *all* covered crops on the farm in the ARC-individual coverage option instead of selecting between PLC and county ARC for each crop.

County ARC

For producers choosing between ARC and PLC on each covered commodity on a farm, the county ARC program has a county revenue guarantee, and only a crop revenue loss at the county level triggers a payment. For ARC county coverage, payments are made on 85% of base acres when actual county crop revenue drops below the county revenue guarantee, which is 86% of historical or "benchmark" revenue. The benchmark revenue per acre is equal to the average historical county yield for the most recent 5 crop years (excluding the years with the highest and lowest yields, or "Olympic average") times the national average market price received by producers during the 12-month marketing year for the most recent 5 crop years (excluding the years with the highest and lowest prices). With the guarantee set at 86%, the producer absorbs the first 14% of the shortfall, and the government absorbs the next 10% of revenue shortfall. (The per-acre payment rate is capped at 10% of benchmark revenue.) Remaining losses are backstopped by crop insurance if purchased at sufficient coverage levels by the producer and by the marketing assistance loan program.

The county ARC payment formula is 85% *times* the number of base acres *times* the difference between the county revenue guarantee and the actual crop revenue. See *Figure 3* for a graphical interpretation of the formula and *Figure 4* for a hypothetical example for corn.

Individual ARC

Farm level protection is provided if producers enroll *all* covered crops on the farm in the ARC-individual coverage option, which uses individual farm yields for each covered crop (which are more variable than county averages) and aggregates all crop revenue into a single, whole-farm guarantee. Individual coverage was not available for ACRE in the 2008 farm bill; farm-level coverage was provided instead by the Supplemental Revenue Assistance (SURE) disaster program (not reauthorized under the 2014 farm bill).

The individual ARC payment formula is 65% *times* the number of total base acres for the farm *times* the difference between the revenue guarantee and the actual crop revenue. The calculation for the guarantee and actual revenue are based on the aggregation of all covered crops on the farm using individual farm yields instead of county yields.[12]

(payment when actual county-wide revenue drops below 86% of historical revenue ["shallow loss"])

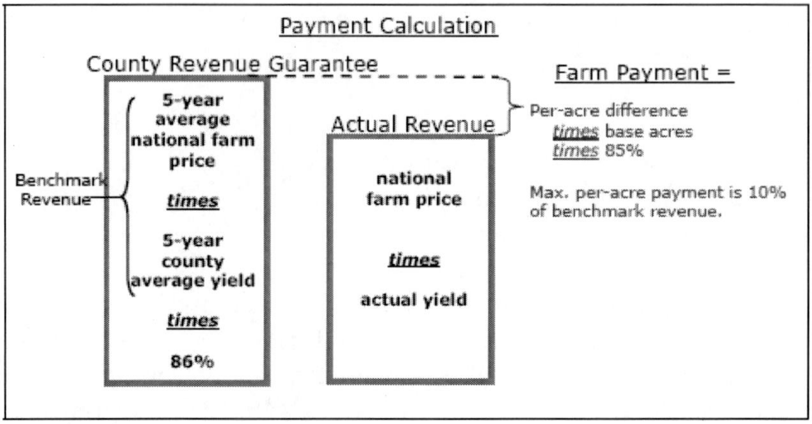

Source: CRS.

Notes: Five-year averages exclude high and low years. Instead of an ARC county guarantee on a crop-by-crop basis, farmers can select a farm-level guarantee for all covered crops on a farm. Payment acreage is reduced to 65% of base acres, and a single, whole farm guarantee (and payment) is calculated as a weighted average for all crops (i.e., not on a crop-by-crop basis).

Figure 3. Agriculture Risk Coverage (ARC)–County Coverage.

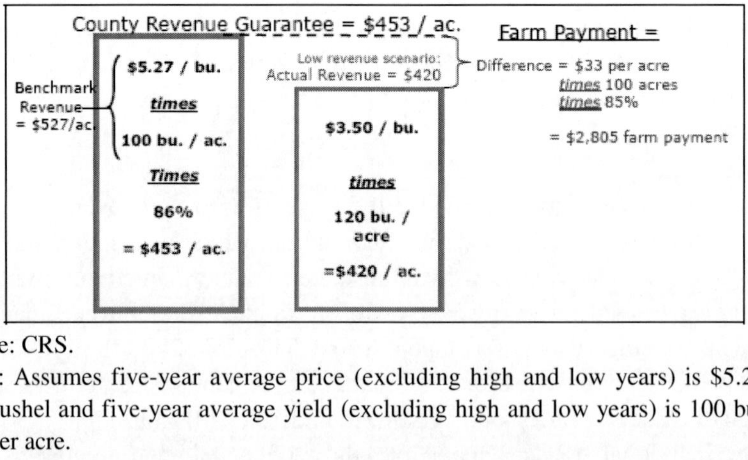

Source: CRS.

Notes: Assumes five-year average price (excluding high and low years) is $5.27 per bushel and five-year average yield (excluding high and low years) is 100 bushels per acre.

Figure 4. Agriculture Risk Coverage (ARC)–Low Revenue Scenario for Corn.

Marketing Assistance Loan Program

The Marketing Assistance Loan (MAL) program provides additional financial benefits to farmers in the form of a guaranteed floor price for qualifying field crops, in addition to providing short-term financing. The process begins with a government loan to participating farmers of designated crops (covered commodities, plus upland cotton, extra long staple cotton, wool, mohair, and honey). The loan is made at a specified "per-unit" loan rate using the crop as collateral. This loan rate, in effect, establishes a price guarantee. Prior to loan maturity, if the local market price (called the "posted price") is at or above the loan rate, the farmer repays the loan principal and interest.[13] In contrast, when the posted price is below the loan rate, the farmer may repay the loan at that price (called the "loan repayment rate") and pocket the difference as a "marketing loan gain."[14] Or, rather than taking the loan when the posted price is below the loan rate, farmers may request a "loan deficiency payment," with the payment rate equal to the difference between the loan rate and the loan repayment rate.

Program benefits are available on the entire crop produced, which means a farmer receives no benefits in the event of a crop loss. This is in contrast to the other two programs (PLC and ARC) that make payments on historical acres and yields and therefore are not dependent on current production.

In the 2014 farm bill, for 2014-2018 crop years, loan rates remain the same as prior law except for upland cotton (see *Table 1* for loan rates). The loan rate for upland cotton is changed from $0.52 per lb. to the simple average of the adjusted prevailing world price for the two immediately preceding marketing years, but not less than $0.45 per pound or more than $0.52 per pound.

Given recent relatively high price levels, the MAL program has paid only limited benefits in recent years for most crops. As a result, some farmers have criticized loan rates as being too low relative to prevailing market prices. MAL program benefits, combined with payments under PLC and ARC, are subject to a payment limit of $125,000 per person for all covered commodities (except peanuts, which has a separate limit of $125,000). Benefits derived from loan forfeitures are exempt from the limit. The 2008 farm bill did not have a payment limit for MAL.

Cotton Not Eligible for Either PLC or ARC

Beginning with the 2014 farm bill, cotton is no longer a covered commodity and not eligible for PLC/ARC payments. Instead it is eligible for a new crop insurance policy called Stacked Income Protection or STAX. Cotton remains eligible for MAL but the loan rate was altered slightly as specified above.

The policy revision was sought by U.S. cotton producers in an attempt to resolve a long-running trade dispute with Brazil that requires changing the U.S. cotton support program so it does not distort international markets.[15] As part of the transition, farm payments are made for upland cotton for the 2014 crop year, and for 2015 if STAX is not available. Payment acres in 2014 equal 60% of 2013 cotton base acres and 36.5% of 2013 cotton base acres in 2015.

Separately, the 2014 farm bill specifies that upon resolution of the trade dispute, funds paid by the U.S. government to Brazil (as part of an agreement made in 2010) may be used for research conducted collaboratively between Brazil and USDA research agencies or with a college, university, or research foundation located in the United States. Among several provisions, the agreement required annual payments of $147.3 million from the United States (via the Commodity Credit Corporation, CCC) to Brazil in order to provide technical assistance and capacity-building for Brazil's cotton sector, but it explicitly excluded funding research.

Planting Fruits and Vegetables on Base Acres

Any crop may be planted without effect on base acres. However, payment acres on a farm are reduced in any crop year in which fruits, vegetables (other than mung beans and pulse crops), or wild rice have been planted on more than 15% of base acres (or 35% in the case of the individual coverage option for ARC). The reduction to payment acres is one-for-one for every acre in excess of these percentages. This allows a limited amount of fruits and vegetables without penalty. Unlike in the past when the reduction in payment acres began at the first acre of fruits and vegetables on base acres, the 2014 farm bill allows 15% (or 35% for individual ARC) of base acres to be planted to fruits and vegetables before the reduction in payment acres begins.

Payment Limits

The enacted 2014 farm bill sets a $125,000 per person cap on the total of PLC, ARC, marketing loan gains and loan deficiency payments. The limit applies to the total from all covered commodities except peanuts, with a separate $125,000 limit for peanuts (for both, limits are doubled with a spouse). This is in contrast to the 2008 farm bill, which had applied limits for each program, specifically $40,000 per person for direct payments, $65,000 for counter-cyclical and ACRE payments, and no limit on marketing loan gain or LDPs.

"Actively Engaged"

To be eligible for payments, persons must be "actively engaged" in farming. Actively engaged, in general, is defined as making a significant contribution of (i) capital, equipment or land, and (ii) personal labor or active personal management. Also, profits are to be commensurate with the level of contributions, and contributions must be at risk. Legal entities can be actively engaged if members collectively contribute personal labor or active personal management. Special classes allow landowners to be considered actively engaged if they receive income based on the farm's operating results, without providing labor or management. Under the 2008 farm bill, spouses were considered actively engaged if the other spouse meets the qualification, allowing payment limits to be doubled.

The 2014 farm bill instructs USDA to write regulations that define "significant contribution of active personal management" to more clearly and objectively implement existing law. The regulation is to apply beginning with the 2015 crop year, and entities made solely of family members are exempt. This final provision differs from earlier Senate-passed and House-passed versions of the 2014 farm bill, which would have deleted "active personal management" and effectively required personal labor in the farming operation. The final 2014 farm bill provision instructs USDA to consider different limits for varying types of farming operations, based on considerations of size, nature, and management requirements of different farming types, changes in the nature of active personal management due to advancements in farming practices, and the impact of this regulation on the long-term viability of farming operations.

Adjusted Gross Income (AGI) Limit

To qualify for any commodity program benefits, recipients must pass an eligibility requirement based on adjusted gross income (AGI) used for federal taxes. The enacted 2014 farm bill establishes the AGI limit as a single, total AGI limit of $900,000 (using a three-year average). In contrast, the 2008 farm bill had two separate limits—farm and non-farm. The non-farm AGI limit was $500,000 to qualify for and receive any farm commodity program benefits, Milk Income Loss Contract (MILC) program, noninsured crop assistance (NAP), or disaster payments. The second limit was $750,000 on farm AGI to receive direct payments.

Some individuals who previously qualified for farm program payments might no longer qualify due to the lower overall limit ($900,000 compared with the combined 2008 farm bill limits of $500,000 and $750,000). However, others might regain eligibility if nonfarm income is high (i.e., between the previous non-farm limit of $500,000 and the new total limit of $900,000) and farm income is low enough to prevent total AGI from exceeding the 2014 farm bill AGI limit of $900,000.

Interaction with Federal Crop Insurance

Federal crop insurance intersects with farm programs when producers choose between the Agriculture Risk Coverage (ARC) and the Price Loss Coverage (PLC) programs. The ARC program is a "shallow loss" program that makes a payment when actual crop revenue is more than 14% below the ARC guarantee. For producers who select the PLC, "shallow loss" coverage is available by purchasing a new crop insurance product called Supplemental Coverage Option (SCO) authorized in Title XI of the 2014 farm bill. SCO is designed to cover part of the deductible on a producer's underlying crop insurance policy. SCO is not available for those enrolled in ARC.

Estimated Cost of the Commodity Title

Because spending on the farm commodity programs involves market-driven counter-cyclical payments, annual outlays can be highly variable. Figure 5 shows that, from 1990 to 2013, commodity program outlays (including dairy programs and disaster payments) were about $5 billion both at the beginning and the end of this period. The high was $27 billion in 2000 when Congress authorized a large sum of "market loss assistance" payments in response to significant price declines in the crop sector. The average over the entire period was $10.1 billion per year.

In January 2014, the Congressional Budget Office (CBO) estimated that for the 2014-2023 period, farm commodity (and disaster program) spending will be $4.4 billion annually, well below the historical averages due to the elimination of direct payments and relatively strong market prices projected by CBO. Given the counter-cyclical design of farm programs, if commodity prices are higher than projected, government outlays will be below projected levels (and vice versa).

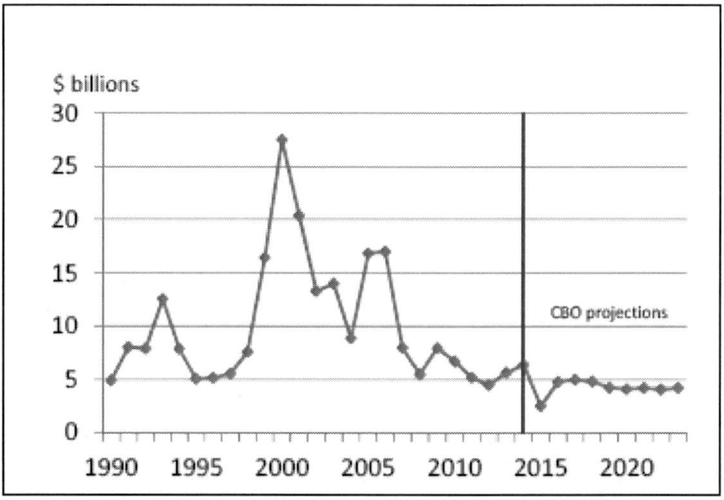

Source: CRS, using USDA (historical data) and CBO data (projections).

Notes: 2013 and prior years are actual outlays from USDA "Table 35, CCC Net Outlays by Commodity and Function," http://www.fsa.usda.gov/Internet/FSA_File/ pb14_ table_35x.xls., summation of rows for covered commodities and loan commodities, dairy, and disaster assistance; 2014-2023 are estimates based on the CBO May 2013 baseline projections for Title I plus CBO 2014 farm bill score for Title I, January 28, 2014.

Figure 5. Outlays for Farm Commodity Program and Disaster Assistance.

Compared to the baseline of continuing the provisions of the 2008 farm bill, the CBO cost estimate (score) of the new provisions in Title I of the farm bill represents five-year savings of $6.3 billion and 10-year savings of $14.3

billion (both relative to baseline projections made in May 2013). If the scores of these changes are added to the 2013 baseline of budget outlays used to write the farm bill, then CBO's expected cost of Title I is $23.6 billion for FY2014-2018 and $44.5 billion over 10 years (*Table 2*). This includes the program crop commodities, dairy, disaster programs, and sugar (no program change).

The 5- and 10-year savings that are scored for all of Title I are the net result of various provisions that either score savings or cost more than prior law. The savings is the result of the elimination of direct, counter-cyclical, and ACRE payments. Also, payments for PLC/ARC are made with a one-year lag, which shifts about $3 billion of payments into a later fiscal year. This achieves savings in the 10-year budget window but does not reduce the total amount eventually paid to farmers. Some of the Title I savings are offset with costs of the new PLC and ARC programs, transition payments to producers of upland cotton (not eligible for PLC/ARC), reauthorized disaster programs, and a revised dairy program.

Table 2. Cost of Provisions in the Commodity Title of the 2014 Farm Bill (in millions of dollars)

Description	5 years: FY2014-FY2018	10 years: FY2014-FY2023
CBO baseline, May 2013, Title I	29,888	58,765
CBO score of changes in Title I of the 2014 farm bill		
Provisions with net savings:		
Repeal direct payments	-18,153	-40,845
Repeal counter-cyclical payments	-489	-1,519
Repeal Average Crop Revenue Election payments	-2,494	-4,718
Provisions with net additional costs:		
Price Loss Coverage	5,115	13,124
Agriculture Risk Coverage	6,528	14,108
Transition payments to producers of upland cotton	558	558
Nonrecourse Marketing Assistance Loans	23	48
Dairy program	241	912
Supplemental Agriculture Disaster Assistance	2,166	3,674
Implementation	120	120
Loan implementation	54	230
Subtotal: CBO Score of 2014 Farm Bill changes, Title I	-6,332	-14,307
CBO Estimate of Total Cost of Title I	23,556	44,458

Source: CBO baseline and score of the conference agreement of H.R. 2642, the Agricultural Act of 2014, as reported on January 27, 2014.

IMPLEMENTATION

The 2014 farm bill provides $100 million to carry out Title I. A portion of the total ($3 million) is marked for educating producers on new commodity, dairy, and disaster programs; and $3 million for web-based program decision tools to help producers make their farm program choices (base reallocations, yield updates, PLC vs. ARC). Congress emphasized the importance of the Acreage Crop Reporting and Streamlining Initiative by making available an additional $10 million if USDA makes sufficient progress by September 2014 and another $10 million if it is fully implemented by September 30, 2015. USDA and university extension service offices have begun publishing information on the 2014 farm bill programs.[16]

USDA announced in late February 2014 that the department intends to issue the regulations for PLC and ARC in the fall of 2014.[17] Once the regulations are in place, USDA indicates that producers can then update producer information and make program choices by late 2014 and early 2015. By then, producers will likely have a general indication about 2014 crop prices, and which program (PLC or ARC) will result in a higher farm payment. The decision is irrevocable for the life of the 2014 farm bill, so producers will need to consider not just 2014 prices, but also expected prices through 2018. Also, wheat farmers can enroll in the Supplemental Coverage Option policy (authorized in the 2014 farm bill) but can later opt out if they select ARC.

APPENDIX. MAJOR FARM COMMODITY PROVISIONS IN THE ENACTED 2014 FARM BILL

Table A-1. Major Farm Commodity Provisions in the 2008 Farm Bill and 2014 Farm Bill

Prior Law: 2008 Farm Bill (P.L. 110-246)	Current Law: 2014 Farm Bill (P.L. 113-79)
Program suspension	
Suspends the permanent price support authority of the Agricultural Adjustment Act of 1938 and the Agricultural Adjustment Act of 1949 for the 2008-13 crop years (covered commodities, peanuts, and sugar), and for milk through December 31, 2013. [7 U.S.C. 8782]	Same as prior law, except applies to 2014-2018 crop years, and through December 31, 2018 for milk. [Sec. 1602]

Table A-1. (Continued)

Prior Law: 2008 Farm Bill (P.L. 110-246)	Current Law: 2014 Farm Bill (P.L. 113-79)
Direct payments (DPs) are available to producers on farms with base acres (historical	Repeals direct payments. [Sec. 1101]
plantings) of covered commodities (wheat, corn, grain sorghum, barley, oats, upland cotton, rice, soybeans, and other oilseeds). [7 U.S.C. 8713] Covers 2008-2013 crop years. Direct payment rates are fixed in statute [7 U.S.C. 7913(b)] and do not vary based on market price. Payment amount = direct payment rate, times 85% of base acres [7 U.S.C. 7911], times direct payment yield [7 U.S.C. 7912]. (Exception: payment acreage is 83.3% of base acres for crop years 2009-2011.) Direct payments for peanuts authorized separately. [7 U.S.C. 8753]	Transition payments are made available for upland cotton for the 2014 crop year. Payment i also made for upland cotton 2015 if STAX crop insurance authorized in Title XI is not available. [Sec. 1119]
Counter-cyclical payments (CCPs) are available for covered commodities for 2008-2013 crop years. [7 U.S.C. 8714] Payment rate is difference between target price in statute (see below) and national average market price (or loan rate, if higher), minus the direct payment rate. Counter-cyclical payments for peanuts authorized separately. [7 U.S.C. 8754(a)(1)-(3)]	Repeals counter-cyclical payments. [Sec. 1102]
For covered commodities and peanuts, Average Crop Revenue Election (ACRE) payments are available to producers as an alternative to CCPs. Revenue payment based on a two-part trigger: (1) if actual state revenue is less than a guaranteed state level for the commodity, and (2) if actual farm revenue is less than a farm ACRE benchmark for the commodity. Payment amount equals the product of (1) the lesser of (a) the ACRE program guarantee minus actual state revenue or (b) 25% of the ACRE program guarantee, times (2) 83.3% (for crop years 2009-2011) or 85% (2012-2013) of the acreage planted of the covered commodity (not to exceed base acres of the commodity), times (3) the 5-year Olympic average farm yield divided by the 5-year Olympic average state yield (Olympic average drops lowest and highest year). For producers who participate in ACRE, loan rates under the marketing assistance loan program are reduced 30% and direct payments are reduced by 20%. [7 U.S.C. 8715]	Repeals Average Crop Revenue Election (ACRE) program. [Sec. 1103]
No comparable definition. However, the terms "actual state revenue" and "actual farm revenue" were used in the Average Crop Revenue Election (ACRE) program (see below).	Actual crop revenue: the amount determined by the Secretary of Agriculture (the Secretary) under the Agriculture Risk Coverage program in Section 1117(b) for each covered commodity for a crop year. [Sec. 1111(1)]
No comparable definition.	Agriculture Risk Coverage (ARC): "shallow loss" revenue coverage provided under

Prior Law: 2008 Farm Bill (P.L. 110-246)	Current Law: 2014 Farm Bill (P.L. 113-79)
	Section 1117. [Sec. 1111(2)]
No comparable definition. However, the term "ACRE program guarantee" was used in the Average Crop Revenue Election (ACRE) program (see below).	Agriculture Risk Coverage (ARC) Guarantee: the amount determined under the Agriculture Risk Coverage program in Section 1117(c). [Sec. 1111(3)]
Base acres: The number of base acres of a covered commodity on a farm as established under the 2002 farm bill [7 U.S.C. 7911], subject to adjustments for pulse crops, other oilseeds, and conservation reserve contracts. [7 U.S.C. 8711] Same for peanuts. [7 U.S.C. 7952, 7 U.S.C. 8752]	Base acres: Individual crop-specific base acreages (except cotton) are retained, as in effect on September 30, 2013, subject to any adjustments in Sec. 1112, including conservation reserve contracts and inclusion of additional oilseeds designated by the Secretary. The term ''base acres'' includes any generic base acres planted to a covered commodity as determined in Section 1114(b). [Sec. 1111(4)]
No comparable definition.	County coverage: type of coverage under the Agriculture Risk Coverage (ARC) program under Section 1115(b)(1) to be obtained by the producer at the county level. [Sec. 1111(5)]
Covered commodities: wheat, corn, grain sorghum, barley, oats, upland cotton, long grain rice, medium grain rice, pulse crops (dry peas, lentils, small chickpeas, and large chickpeas), soybeans, and other oilseeds (sunflower seed, rapeseed, canola, safflower, flaxseed, mustard seed, crambe, sesame seed). [7 U.S.C. 7901(4,9) Peanuts were not defined as a "covered commodity" but treated as such under farm programs.	Similar to previous law except upland cotton is removed and peanuts are added to the list of covered commodities. Also, acreage of wheat, oats, and barley used for haying and grazing is eligible. [Sec. 1111(6)]
Effective price: the higher of (1) the national season average market price or (2) national average loan rate plus the direct payment rate. [7 U.S.C. 7914(b)] Same provision for peanuts. [7 U.S.C. 7954(b)]	Effective price: for a covered commodity for a crop year, the price calculated by the Secretary under Section 1116(b) to determine whether Price Loss Coverage (PLC) payments are required for that crop year. [Sec. 1111(7)] The effective price is the higher of (1) the national average market price received by producers during the 12-month marketing year for the covered commodity, as determined by the Secretary; or (2) the national average loan rate for a marketing assistance loan. [Sec. 1116(b)] The effective price for barley is the all-barley price. [Sec. 1116(f)].
Extra long staple cotton: cotton that (A) is produced from pure strain varieties of the Barbadense species or any hybrid of the species, or other similar types of extra long staple cotton having characteristics needed for various end uses for which U.S. upland cotton is not suitable, and grown in irrigated or other designated U.S. cotton-growing regions; and (B) is ginned on a roller-type gin or, other authorized gin for experimental	Extra long staple cotton: same as prior law. [Sec. 1111(8)]

Table A-1. (Continued)

Prior Law: 2008 Farm Bill (P.L. 110-246)	Current Law: 2014 Farm Bill (P.L. 113-79)
purposes. [7 U.S.C. 7901(7)]	
No comparable definition.	Generic base acres: the number of base acres for cotton in effect under Section 1001 of the Food, Conservation, and Energy Act of 2008 (7 U.S.C. 8702), as adjusted pursuant to Section 1101 of such Act (7 U.S.C. 8711), as in effect on September 30, 2013, subject to any adjustment or reduction under Section 1112 of this act. [Sec. 1111(9)] Generic base is eligible for payments if a covered crop is planted on the farm (see payment discussion below).
No comparable definition. However, note that under the Supplemental Revenue Assistance (SURE) program [7 U.S.C. 1531], payments compensated producers for a portion of losses at the farm level that was not eligible for an indemnity payment under a crop insurance policy.	Individual coverage: type of coverage under the Agriculture Risk Coverage (ARC) program in Section 1115(b)(1) to be obtained by the producer at the farm level. [Sec. 1111(10)]
Medium grain rice: includes short grain rice. [7 U.S.C. 8702(9)	Medium grain rice: includes short grain rice and temperate japonica rice. [Sec. 1111(11)]
Other oilseed: a crop of sunflower seed, rapeseed, canola, safflower, flaxseed, mustard seed, crambe, sesame seed, or, if designated by the Secretary, another oilseed. [7 U.S.C. 7901(9)]	Other oilseed: same as prior law. [Sec. 1111(12)]
Payment acres: 85% of the base acres of a covered commodity on a farm on which direct payments and counter-cyclical payments are made. Exception: 83.3% of base acres for direct payments only for crop years 2009-2011. [7 U.S.C. 7901(10)]	Payment acres: the number of acres determined for a farm under Section 1114 for Price Loss Coverage payments and Agriculture Risk Coverage payments. [Sec. 1111(13)]
Payment yield: the yield for counter-cyclical program payments under the 2002 farm bill, generally based on 1998-2001 data. [7 U.S.C. 7901(10)]	Payment yield: the yield used to make counter-cyclical payments under the 2008 farm bill as in effect on September 30, 2013; or the yield established under Section 1113 (Price Loss Coverage program) of this act. [Sec. 1111(14)]
No comparable definition.	Price Loss Coverage: price-based coverage provided under Section 1116. [Sec. 1111(15)]
Producer: generally, an owner, operator, landlord, tenant, or sharecropper that shares in the risk of producing a crop and is entitled to share in the crop available for marketing from the farm, or would have shared had the crop been produced. For a grower of hybrid seed, the existence of a hybrid seed contract and other program rules shall not adversely affect the ability to receive a payment. [7U.S.C. 7901(12)]	Producer: same as prior law. [Sec. 1111(16)]
Pulse crop: dry peas, lentils, small chickpeas, and large	Pulse crop: same as prior law. [Sec.

Prior Law: 2008 Farm Bill (P.L. 110-246)	Current Law: 2014 Farm Bill (P.L. 113-79)
chickpeas. [7U.S.C. 8702(14)]	1111(17)]
Target prices for 2013:	Reference prices:
Wheat, bu., $4.17	Wheat, bu., $5.50
Corn, bu., $2.63	Corn, bu., $3.70
Grain sorghum, bu., $2.63	Grain sorghum, bu., $3.95
Barley, bu., $2.63	Barley, bu., $4.95
Oats, bu., $1.79	Oats, bu., $2.40
Upland cotton, lb., $0.7125	Upland cotton, none (covered by STAX program Title XI)
Long grain rice, cwt., $10.50	Long grain rice, cwt., $14.00
Medium grain rice, cwt., $10.50	Medium grain rice, cwt., $14.00
Soybeans, bu., $6.00 Other oilseeds, cwt., $12.68 Dry peas, cwt., $8.32 Lentils, cwt., $12.81 Small chickpeas, cwt., $10.36 Large chickpeas, cwt., $12.81 Peanuts, ton, $495 [7U.S.C. 8714(c)(3)]	—(temperate japonica rice, reference price for PLC is increased an additional 15% to $16.10 per cwt.) [Sec. 1116(g)] Soybeans, bu., $8.40 Other oilseeds, cwt., $20.15 Dry peas, cwt., $11.00 Lentils, cwt., $19.97 Small chickpeas, cwt., $19.04 Large chickpeas, cwt., $21.54 Peanuts, ton, $535 [Sec. 1111(18)]
Secretary: the Secretary of Agriculture. [7 U.S.C. 7901(13)]	Secretary: same as prior law. [Sec. 1111(19)]
State: each of the U.S. States, the District of Columbia, the Commonwealth of Puerto Rico, or U.S. territory/possession. [7 U.S.C. 7901(14)]	State: same as prior law. [Sec. 1111(20)]
No comparable definition.	Temperate japonica rice: rice that is grown in high altitudes or temperate regions of high latitudes with cooler climate conditions, in the Western United States, as determined by the Secretary. [Sec. 1111(21)]
Transitional yield: as defined in section 502(b) of the Federal Crop Insurance Act, the	Transitional yield: same as prior law. [Sec. 1111(22)]
maximum average production per acre or equivalent measure that is assigned to acreage for a crop year by the Federal Crop Insurance Corporation whenever the producer fails to: (A) certify that acceptable documentation of production and acreage for the crop year is in the possession of the producer; or (B) present the acceptable documentation. [7 U.S.C. 1502(b)]	
United States: when used in a geographical sense, all of the States. [7 U.S.C. 7901(16)]	United States: same as prior law. [Sec. 1111(23)]
United States premium factor: the percentage by which the difference in the United	United States premium factor: same as prior law. [Sec. 1111(24)]
States loan schedule premiums for Strict Middling (SM) 1 1/8-inch upland cotton and for Middling (M) 1 3/32-inch upland cotton exceeds the difference in the applicable premiums for comparable international qualities. [7 U.S.C. 8702(18)] Base, Payment Yields, and Payment Acres	

Table A-1. (Continued)

Prior Law: 2008 Farm Bill (P.L. 110-246)	Current Law: 2014 Farm Bill (P.L. 113-79)
Base acres: Unlike 2002 farm bill, no provision in 2008 farm bill for reallocating base acres among crops to reflect recent plantings.	Base acre retention or one-time reallocation: Farm owners have a one-time opportunity to either: (1) retain base acres (including any generic base acres), or (2) reallocate base acres (other than any generic base acres) among covered crops to reflect recent historical planting shares equal to the 4-year average (2009-2012) planted area for each covered crop (including prevented plant acreage). Additional provisions: all four years are included in the average (even if zero); with multiple plantings per years, only one crop may be used in the calculation; reallocation of base acres among covered commodities may not result in an increase in total base acres (including generic base). [Sec. 1112(a)]
Accommodations for double cropping and CRP acres. Base cannot exceed total cropland. [7 U.S.C. 7911]	Similar to prior law, including provision to increase/decrease base when land leaves/enters conservation programs. [Sec. 1112(b)] However, base is reduced if the sum of the base acres for the farm (including any new oilseed acreage and generic base acres) plus any acreage in CRP or the Wetlands Reserve Program (or other federal conservation program that makes payments in exchange for not producing a crop) exceeds the actual cropland acreage on the farm. [Sec. 1112(c)] Base is reduced proportionately when acreage has been subdivided and developed for multiple residential units or other non-farming uses. [Sec. 1112(d)]
Payment yields: Established direct payment yields for designated oilseeds, camelina, or pulse crops using 1998-2001 farm yields, adjusted back to the national average from 1981-85. For counter-cyclical payments, yield could be updated to reflect yields during 1998-2001 using specific formulas. [7 U.S.C. 7912]	Payment yields: For Price Loss Coverage payments under Section 1116, the Secretary shall establish a yield for each farm for any designated oilseed for which a payment yield was not established under Section 1102 of the 2008 farm bill. If the yield per planted acre for a crop of a designated oilseed for a farm for any of the 1998 through 2001 crop years was less than 75% of the county yield for that designated oilseed, the Secretary shall assign a yield for that crop year equal to 75% of the county yield. [Sec. 1113(a-c)]
No comparable provision.	Updating payment yields for Price Loss Coverage (PLC): The owner of a farm

Prior Law: 2008 Farm Bill (P.L. 110-246)	Current Law: 2014 Farm Bill (P.L. 113-79)
	has a 1-time opportunity to update, on a covered commodity-by-covered-commodity basis, the payment yield used in calculating PLC payments for each covered commodity. The PLC payment yield is equal to 90% of the average of the yield per planted acre for the crop of the covered commodity for the 2008 through 2012 crop years, excluding any crop year in which the acreage planted to the crop of the covered commodity was zero. If the yield for any of the 2008 through 2012 crop years was less than 75% of the average county yield during that period, a "plug" yield for that crop year is equal to 75% of the county average for 2008 through 2012. ***[Sec. 1113(d)]***
Payment acres: 85% of the base acres of a covered commodity on a farm on which direct payments and counter-cyclical payments are made. Exception: 83.3% of base acres for direct payments only for crop years 2009-2011. [7 U.S.C. 7901(10)]	Payment acres: For Price Loss Coverage (PLC) and the Agriculture Risk Coverage (ARC) when county coverage has been selected, the number of payment acres for each covered commodity on a farm is equal to 85% of the base acres for the covered commodity. In the case of ARC when individual coverage has been selected, the payment acreage is equal to 65% of the base acres for all of the covered commodities on the farm. [Sec. 1114(a)] Payment acres may not include any crop subsequently planted during the same crop year on the same land for which the first crop is eligible for PLC payments or ARC payments, unless the crop was approved for double cropping in the county, as determined by the Secretary. [Sec. 1114(c)] Generic base is eligible for payments if a covered crop is planted on the farm. Specifically, for each crop year, generic base acres are attributed (i.e. temporarily designated as) base acres to a particular covered commodity base in proportion to that crop's share of total plantings of all covered commodities in that year. The amount of generic base attributed for a particular year cannot exceed the acreage planted to covered crops in that year. In other words, if the total number of acres planted to all covered commodities on the farm does not exceed the generic base acres on the farm, only the amount of acreage actually planted to a covered commodity is

Table A-1. (Continued)

Prior Law: 2008 Farm Bill (P.L. 110-246)	Current Law: 2014 Farm Bill (P.L. 113-79)
	attributed to that covered commodity for payment purposes. [Sec. 1114(b)]
Farms with limited base acres: A producer on a farm may not receive direct payments, counter-cyclical payments, or average crop revenue election payments (see below) if the sum of the base acres of the farm is 10 acres or less (provision was suspended for the 2008 crop year only). [7 U.S.C. 8711(d)]	Minimal payment acres: A producer on a farm may not receive Price Loss Coverage payments or Agriculture Risk Coverage payments (see below) if the sum of the base acres on the farm is 10 acres or less, except for socially disadvantaged farmers/ranchers or limited resource farmers/ranchers, [Sec. 1114(d)]
Planting flexibility: Any crop may be planted on base acres to receive program benefits, except fruits, vegetables (other than mung beans and pulse crops), and wild rice. Exceptions provide for farms and producers with a history of double-cropping or history of growing fruits and vegetables; in this case, direct and counter-cyclical payments are reduced acre-for-acre for the year. [7 U.S.C. 8717, 7 U.S.C. 8756] A pilot program beginning in 2009 in seven Midwestern states allowed planting of fruits and vegetables for processing on base acres. Base acres were temporarily reduced for the year, but restored for the next crop year and "considered planted" for any future base calculations. [7 U.S.C. 8717(d)]	Effect of planting fruits and vegetables: Any crop may be planted without effect on base acres. However, payment acres on a farm are reduced in any crop year in which fruits, vegetables (other than mung beans and pulse crops), or wild rice have been planted on base acres. The reduction to payment acres is one-for-one for each acre planted to these crops in excess of 15% of base acres for either the Price Loss Coverage or county coverage under the Agriculture Risk Coverage (ARC) program, and in excess of 35% of base acres for ARC individual coverage. [Sec. 1114(e)]
Producer election: Producers may choose between the Counter-cyclical payments (CCPs) and Average Crop Revenue Election (ACRE) payments. If CCP was selected, direct payments were reduced 20% and marketing loan rates are reduced by 30%. Producers can enter ACRE any year of the 2009-2012 crop years, but cannot return to the traditional counter-cyclical program. [7 U.S.C. 8715(a)(1)] If all of the producers on a farm fail to make an election or make different elections, all of the producers on the farm are deemed to have made the election to receive counter-cyclical payments. [7 U.S.C. 8715(a)(5)] After the 2008 farm bill was extended by 1 year by the American Taxpayer Relief Act of 2012, producers were offered the same choice for the 2013 crop year.	Producer election: For the 2014 through 2018 crop years, all of the producers on a farm shall make a one-time, irrevocable election to obtain either Price Loss Coverage on a covered commodity-by-covered-commodity basis; or Agriculture Risk Coverage. [Sec. 1115(a)] For ARC, producers must unanimously select whether to receive ARC payments based on: (1) county coverage applicable on a covered-commodity-by-covered-commodity basis; or (2) individual coverage applicable to all of the covered commodities on the farm. [Sec. 1115(b)] If all the producers on a farm fail to make a unanimous election for the 2014 crop year, no program payments are made to the farm for the 2014 crop year and the producers on the farm shall be deemed to have elected PLC for all covered commodities on the farm for the 2015 through 2018 crop years. [Sec. 1115(c)] If all the producers on a farm select ARC county coverage for a covered commodity,

Prior Law: 2008 Farm Bill (P.L. 110-246)	Current Law: 2014 Farm Bill (P.L. 113-79)
	the Secretary cannot make PLC payments to the producers on the farm with respect to that covered commodity. [Sec. 1115(d)] If all the producers on a farm select individual coverage, payment calculations include the producer's share of all farms in the same state in which the producer has an interest and for which individual coverage has been selected. [Sec. 1115(e)] Producers on a farm cannot reconstitute the farm to void or change a program election. [Sec. 1115(f)]
Price-Based Payments	
Counter-cyclical payments (CCPs) are available for covered commodities for 2008-2013 crop years when the farm price is below the effective price (target price in statute minus the direct payment rate). [7 U.S.C. 8714] Payment rate is the difference between target price in statute and the national 12-month average farm price (or loan rate, if higher), minus the direct payment rate. Counter-cyclical payments for peanuts authorized separately. [7 U.S.C. 8754(a)(1)-(3)] Payment amount = Payment rate times 85% of base acres times counter-cyclical program yield for the farm (generally based on 1998-2001 data). [7 U.S.C. 7912]	Repeals counter-cyclical payments. [Sec. 1102] Establishes similar program called Price Loss Coverage (PLC) for crop years 2014-18. PLC payments are made on a farm on a covered commodity-by-covered-commodity basis if the effective price (the higher of the national average 12-month market price or the loan rate) is less than the reference price. Payment rate is the difference between the reference price in statute and the national 12-month average market price (or loan rate, if higher). [Sec. 1116] Payment amount = Payment rate times 85% of base acres for each covered commodity (including attributed generic base) times existing counter-cyclical program yield (or updated yields equal to 90% of 2008-2012 average yield per planted acre). [Sec. 1116(d)] (See Sec. 1113 for more on payment yields.) Payments shall be made beginning October 1, or as soon as practicable thereafter, after the end of the applicable marketing year for the covered commodity. [Sec. 1116(e)]
Revenue-Based Payments	
For covered commodities and peanuts, Average Crop Revenue Election (ACRE) payments are available to producers as an alternative to CCPs. [7 U.S.C. 8715]	Repeals Average Crop Revenue Election (ACRE) program. [Sec. 1103] Establishes similar program called Agriculture Risk Coverage (ARC) as an alternative to PLC payments for crop years 2014-18 on a commodity-by-commodity basis for each farm (except when producers select individual (farm) ARC, then PLC is not an option for any commodity). Producers select either county coverage or individual farm coverage. [Sec. 1117]
Revenue payment based on a two-part trigger: (1) if the actual state revenue is less than a guaranteed state level	Revenue payment based on single trigger: if the actual crop revenue is less than the

Table A-1. (Continued)

Prior Law: 2008 Farm Bill (P.L. 110-246)	Current Law: 2014 Farm Bill (P.L. 113-79)
for the commodity, and (2) if actual farm revenue is less than a farm ACRE benchmark for the commodity. [7 U.S.C. 8715(b)(2)]	agriculture risk coverage guarantee. [Sec. 1117(a)]
Actual state revenue per acre = actual state yield, times the national average market price. Actual state yield is the actual quantity produced in the state during the crop year, divided by planted acres. [7 U.S.C. 8715(c)] National average market price is the greater of the national average price received during the 12-month marketing year, or the marketing loan rate after being reduced by 30%. [7 U.S.C. 8715(a)(1)] Actual farm revenue per acre = actual farm yield, times the greater of the national average price received during the 12-month marketing year or the marketing loan rate after being reduced by 30%. [7 U.S.C. 8715(e)]	In the case of county coverage, actual crop revenue per acre = the actual average county yield per planted acre for the covered commodity times the higher of (i) the national average market price received by producers during the 12-month marketing year, or (ii) the national average loan rate. [Sec. 1117(b)(1)] In the case of individual (farm) coverage, actual crop revenue per acre is the producer's share of the aggregated revenue amount for all covered commodities planted on all farms for which individual coverage has been selected. Actual crop revenue is equal to the sum of covered commodity revenue (total production of each covered commodity on such farms, times the higher of (i) the national average market price received by producers during the 12-month marketing year, or (ii) the national average loan rate) divided by the total planted acres of all covered commodities on such farms. [Sec. 1117(b)(2)]
ACRE program guarantee per acre = 90% times the benchmark state yield, times the ACRE program guarantee price. [7 U.S.C. 8715(d)] The benchmark state yield is a 5-year Olympic average state yield. [7 U.S.C. 8715(d)(2)(A)] The ACRE program guarantee price is a 2-year average of the national average market price. [7 U.S.C. 8715(d)(3)]The ACRE program guarantee cannot change more than 10% from the previous year. [7 U.S.C. 8715(d)(1)(B)] Farm ACRE benchmark revenue per acre = the 5-year Olympic average farm yield, times the ACRE program guarantee price; plus the crop insurance premium per acre. [7 U.S.C. 8715(f)]	ARC guarantee per acre = 86% times the benchmark revenue. [Sec. 1117(c)(1)] In the case of county coverage, benchmark revenue per acre = the average historical county yield for the most recent 5 crop years (excluding the years with the highest and lowest yields, or "Olympic average") times the national Olympic average market price received by producers during the 12-month marketing year for the most recent 5 crop years. [Sec. 1117(c)(2)] In the case of individual coverage, benchmark revenue is based on the producer's share of all covered commodities planted on all farms for which individual coverage has been selected and in which the producer has an interest. Benchmark revenue is the summation of Olympic 5-year average benchmark revenue for each covered commodity aggregated across all farms with individual coverage, adjusted to reflect

Prior Law: 2008 Farm Bill (P.L. 110-246)	Current Law: 2014 Farm Bill (P.L. 113-79)
	current-year planted acreage. Annual revenue for each covered commodity is equal to the farm yield per planted acre for the covered commodity, times the national average market price received by producers during the 12-month marketing year. [Sec. 1117(c)(3)] If the yield per planted acre for the covered commodity or historical county yield per planted acre for the covered commodity for any of the 5 most recent crop years is less than 70% of the transitional yield, the amounts used for any of those years is equal to 70% of the transitional yield. *[Sec. 1117(c)(4)]* The reference price is used if the national average farm price for any of the 5 most recent cropyears is lower than the reference price. *[Sec. 1117(c)(5)]*
If more than 25% of a state's acreage is irrigated and 25% is non-irrigated, separate guarantees shall apply. [7 U.S.C. 8715(d)(4)] Payment amount = the product of (1) the lesser of (a) the ACRE program guarantee minus actual state revenue or (b) 25% of the ACRE program guarantee, times (2) 83.3% (2009-2011) or 85% (2012 and 2013) of the acreage planted of the covered commodity (not to exceed base acres of the commodity), times (3) the 5- year Olympic average farm yield divided by the 5-year Olympic average state yield. This formula multiplies a state-level payment rate per acre (up to a maximum of 25% of the guarantee level) times a percentage of planted acreage, then prorates the payment based on the farm's yield history compared to the state's yield history. [7 U.S.C. 8715(g)] For producers who participate in ACRE, loan rates under the marketing assistance loan program are reduced 30% and direct payments are reduced by 20%. [7 U.S.C. 8715(a)(1)] Timing: Beginning October 1 after the end of the marketing year. [7 U.S.C. 8715(b)(3)] No comparable provision.	To the maximum extent practicable, calculate separate ARC guarantees for irrigated and nonirrigated covered commodities. [Sec. 1117(g)(2)] The payment rate for a covered commodity, in the case of county coverage, or a farm, in the case of individual coverage, is equal to the lesser of: (1) the amount that the ARC guarantee for the crop year exceeds the actual crop revenue for the crop year, or (2) 10% of the benchmark revenue for the crop year. [Sec. 1117(d)] Payment amount = the payment rate times the payment acres. For county coverage, payment acres = 85% of the base acres for the covered commodity. For individual coverage, payment acreage = 65% of the base acres for all of the covered commodities on the farm. [Sec. 1117(e)] Timing: Beginning October 1after the end of the marketing year. [Sec. 1117(f)] Additional duties of the Secretary: Use all available information and analysis, including data mining, to check for anomalies in the determination of ARC payments; if necessary, assign an average yield for a farm or county on the basis of the yield history representative of the area. [Sec. 1117(g)]
Conservation Compliance/Producer Agreement	
Eligibility for direct payments, counter-cyclical payments, or average crop revenue election payments requires producers to comply with conservation,	Similar to prior law, with application to the new Price Loss Coverage (PLC) and Agriculture Risk Coverage (ARC) programs,

Table A-1. (Continued)

Prior Law: 2008 Farm Bill (P.L. 110-246)	Current Law: 2014 Farm Bill (P.L. 113-79)
wetland, and planting flexibility requirements; use base acres for agricultural or conserving use, and not for nonagricultural commercial, industrial, or residential use; control noxious weeds and maintain sound agricultural practices. Producers must submit annual acreage reports for all cropland on the farm; for those who receive ACRE payment, annual production reports are also required. [7 U.S.C. 8716(a)(c)] Same provision for peanuts (except production report requirement). [7 U.S.C. 8755(a)(c)] Under Title II (Conservation) of the 2008 farm bill (P.L. 110-246), benefits under the marketing loan program are subject to conservation compliance for highly erodible land [16 U.S.C. 3811(a)(1)(A)] and for Swampbuster [16 U.S.C. 3812(a)(1)]. Sets requirements for transfer of interest in base acres. Protects interests of tenants and sharecroppers and provides for sharing of payments on a farm on an equitable basis. [7 U.S.C. 7915(b)(d)(e)] Same provision for peanuts. [7 U.S.C. 7955(b)(d)(e)]	and marketing loans. [Sec. 1118(a)] Annual production reports are required for producers selecting individual ARC coverage. [Sec. 1118(c)] No penalties can be assessed against a producer for an inaccurate acreage or production report unless the Secretary determines that the producer knowingly and willfully falsified the report. [Sec. 1118(e)] Separately, in Title II (Conservation), a producer must be in compliance with highly erodible land conservation requirements and wetland requirements in order to receive crop insurance premium subsidies. [Sec. 2609]
Transition Payments	
No comparable provision.	Transition (direct) payments are made for upland cotton for the 2014 crop year, and for 2015 if STAX insurance product (Title XI) is not available.
	Payment equals program yield (divided by the national yield of 597 pounds per acre) times transition assistance rate times payment acres. Transition rate is based on cotton price decline between June 2013 and December 2013. Payment acres in 2014 equal 60% of 2013 cotton base acres and 36.5% in 2015. [Sec. 1119]
Nonrecourse Marketing Loans and Other Recourse Loans	
Nonrecourse marketing loans are available for any amount of a loan commodity (see list below) produced in crop years 2008-2013. [7 U.S.C. 8731] Nonrecourse marketing loans for peanuts are authorized separately. [7 U.S.C. 8757]	Generally continues prior law to cover 2014-2018 crop years for all loan commodities (including peanuts). [Sec. 1201]
For peanuts, nonrecourse marketing loans available in crop years 2008-2013. May be obtained through a marketing cooperative or association approved by USDA. Storage to be provided on a non-discriminatory basis and under any additional requirements. Payment of peanut storage costs authorized for 2008-2013 crops. [7 U.S.C. 8757(a)(4)-(7)]	
Loan commodities and loan rates:	Loan commodities same as prior law. [Sec.

Prior Law: 2008 Farm Bill (P.L. 110-246)	Current Law: 2014 Farm Bill (P.L. 113-79)
	1201]
Wheat, per bushel (bu.), $2.94 ($2.75 in 2008, 2009) Corn, bu., $1.95 Grain sorghum, bu., $1.95 Barley, bu., $1.85 Oats, bu., $1.33 Upland cotton, lb., $0.52 Extra long staple (ELS) cotton, lb., $0.7977 Long grain rice, hundredweight (cwt.), $6.50 Medium grain rice, cwt., $6.50 Soybeans, bu., $5.00 Other oilseeds, cwt., $10.09 ($9.30 in 2008, 2009) Dry peas, cwt., $5.40 ($6.22 in 2008) Lentils, cwt., $11.28 ($11.72 in 2008) Small chickpeas, cwt., $7.43 Large chickpeas, cwt., $11.28 (not applicable in 2008) Graded wool, lb., $1.15 ($1.00 in 2008, 2009) Nongraded wool, lb., $0.40 Mohair, lb., $4.20 Honey, lb., $0.69 ($0.60 in 2008, 2009) [7 U.S.C. 8732 (a)(b)(c)] Peanuts, ton, $355 [7 U.S.C. 8757(b)]	For 2014-2018 crop years, loan rates same as prior law except for upland cotton. The loan rate for upland cotton is changed from $0.52 per lb. to the simple average of the adjusted prevailing world price for the two immediately preceding marketing years, but not less than $0.45 per pound or more than $0.52 per pound. [Sec. 1202]
Establishes a single loan rate in each county for each kind of "other oilseeds" [7 U.S.C. 8732(d)]	
Term of loans: 9 months after the day the loan is made; no extensions. [7 U.S.C. 8733] Same term for peanuts. [7 U.S.C. 8757(c)]	Same as prior law. [Sec. 1203]
Loan repayment: Loans may be repaid at the lesser of (1) the loan rate plus interest, (2) a rate based on average market prices during the preceding 30-day period, or (3) a rate determined by USDA that will minimize forfeitures, accumulation of stocks, storage costs, market impediments, and discrepancies in benefits across states and counties. Excludes upland cotton, rice, ELS cotton, confectionery and each other kind of sunflower seed (other than oil sunflower seed). [7 U.S.C. 8734(a)] Provides USDA authority to temporarily, and on a short-term basis only, adjust the repayment rates in the event of a severe disruption to marketing, transportation or related infrastructure. [7 U.S.C. 8734(h)] Similar provisions for peanuts. [7 U.S.C. 8757(d)] For upland cotton, long grain rice, and medium grain rice, repayment may be at the lesser of the loan rate plus interest, or the prevailing world price for the commodity adjusted to U.S. quality and location. [7 U.S.C. 8734(b)] For ELS cotton, repayment must be at the loan rate plus interest. [7 U.S.C. 8734(c)] For confectionery and other kinds of sunflower seeds (other than oil sunflower seed), loans must be repaid at the lesser of (1) the loan rate plus interest, or (2) the repayment rate for oil	Same as prior law. [Sec. 1204]

Table A-1. (Continued)

Prior Law: 2008 Farm Bill (P.L. 110-246)	Current Law: 2014 Farm Bill (P.L. 113-79)
sunflower seed. [7 U.S.C. 8734(f)]	
For 2008-2011 crop years, USDA provides cotton storage payments at the same rates as provided for the 2006 crop, but reduced by 10%. Beginning with 2012 crop year, the rates are reduced by 20%. [7 U.S.C. 8734(g)]	Cotton storage payments reauthorized for 2014-2018 crop years with 10% rate reduction. [Sec. 1204]
Loan deficiency payments (LDP) are available to producers who agree to forego marketing loans. LDP computed by multiplying the payment rate (the amount that the loan rate exceeds the rate at which a marketing loan may be repaid) for the commodity times the quantity of the commodity produced. Loan deficiency payments available for unshorn pelts or hay and silage, even though they are not eligible for marketing loans. ELS cotton is not eligible. Payment rates determined using the rate in effect as of the date that producers request payment (producers do not need to lose beneficial interest). [7 U.S.C. 8735] Same provision for peanuts. [7 U.S.C. 8757(e)]	For 2014-2018 crop years, same as prior law. [Sec. 1205]
Payments in lieu of LDP for grazed acreage of wheat, barley, oats, or triticale. [7 U.S.C. 8736]	For 2014-2018 crop years, same as prior law, except yield can be based on ARC or PLC if applicable or as determined by the Secretary. [Sec. 1206]
Special marketing loan provisions for upland cotton impose a special import quota on upland cotton through July 31, 2013, when price of U.S. cotton, delivered to a definable and significant international market, exceeds the prevailing world market price for 4 weeks. [7 U.S.C. 8737(a)] Limited global import quota is imposed on upland cotton when U.S. prices average 130% of the previous 3-year average of U.S. prices [7 U.S.C. 8737(b)]	Provisions extended without an expiration date beginning August 1, 2014. [Sec. 1207]
Economic adjustment assistance to users of upland cotton provides assistance to domestic users of upland cotton for uses of all cotton regardless of origin to acquire, construct, install, modernize, develop, convert, or expand land, plant, buildings, equipment, facilities, or machinery. Rate was 4¢/lb. between August 1, 2008, and July 31, 2012, and declined to 3¢/lb. effective beginning August 1, 2012. [7 U.S.C. 8737(c)]	Same as prior law except assistance begins August 1, 2013, at the 3¢/lb. rate. [Sec. 1207]
Special competitiveness program for ELS cotton provides payments to domestic users and exporters whenever the world market price for the lowest priced ELS cotton is below the prevailing U.S. price for a competing growth of ELS cotton for a 4-week period; and the lowest priced competing growth of ELS cotton is less than 134% of the loan rate for ELS cotton.	Same as prior law during the period beginning on the date of enactment of this act through July 31, 2019. [Sec. 1208]

Prior Law: 2008 Farm Bill (P.L. 110-246)	Current Law: 2014 Farm Bill (P.L. 113-79)
Effective through July 31, 2013. [7 U.S.C. 8738]	
Recourse loans for high moisture feed grains and seed cotton are available for farms that normally harvest corn or sorghum in a high moisture condition at rates set by the USDA. For recourse loans for seed cotton, repayment is at loan rate plus interest. [7 U.S.C. 8739]	For 2014-2018 crop years, same as prior law except payment yield for feed grains is the lower of the PLC yield or actual yield. [Sec. 1209]
Adjustments of loan rates are authorized for any commodity (other than cotton) based on differences in grade, type, quality, location, and other factors. Allows county loan rates as low as 95% of the U.S. average, if it does not increase outlays; prohibits adjustments that would increase the national average loan rate. For cotton, loan rates may be adjusted for differences in quality factors. [7 U.S.C. 8740]; [7 U.S.C. 8758] for peanuts.	Same as prior law except removes certain mandatory provisions to quality adjustments. [Sec. 1210]
Payment Limitations	
Establishes the maximum amount of payments per year to a person or legal entity for the sum of all covered commodities, except peanuts. Peanuts have a separate but equal payment limitation. —Direct payments: $40,000 —Direct payments under ACRE: $40,000 minus the reduction required for an ACRE participant. —Counter-cyclical payments: $65,000 —ACRE payments: $65,000 plus the reduction in the limit from the direct payment limit. —Marketing loan gains/LDP: no limit. [7 U.S.C. 1308 (a)-(d)]	Establishes a per-year limit on commodity program payments: Price Loss Coverage (PLC) payment, Agriculture Risk Coverage (ARC) payments, marketing loan gains and LDPs. —PLC, ARC, marketing loan gains and loan deficiency payments, for the sum of all covered commodities except peanuts: $125,000. [Sec. 1603(b)] —PLC, ARC, marketing loan gains and loan deficiency payments, for peanuts: $125,000. [Sec. 1603(c)] —cotton transition payments (2014 and 2015): $40,000. [Sec. 1119(e)]
Payments are attributed to a person by accounting for the direct and indirect ownership in any legal entity. Payments made directly to a person are combined with the person's pro rata share of payments from a legal entity. Payments to a legal entity cannot exceed the limits above, and are attributed to persons. Attribution of payments to legal entities is traced to four levels of ownership. If a payment has not been allocated to an individual after four levels of ownership, the payment to the first-level entity is reduced on a pro-rata basis. [7 U.S.C. 1308 (e)-(h)]	Continues other payment limit provisions such as direct attribution. Addresses active personal management (see below).
To be eligible for payments, persons must be "actively engaged" in farming. Actively engaged, in general, is defined as making a significant contribution of (i) capital, equipment or land, and (ii) personal labor or active personal management. Also, profits are to be commensurate with the level of contributions, and contributions must be at risk. Legal entities can be actively engaged if members collectively contribute personal labor or active personal management. Special classes allow landowners to be considered actively	Does not change the existing statute regarding requirements to be actively engaged in farming; that is, it continues to allow active personal management. However, it instructs the Secretary of Agriculture to write new regulations that define "significant contribution of active personal management" (to more clearly and objectively implement 7 U.S.C 1308-1(b)(2), recognizing past difficulties).

Table A-1. (Continued)

Prior Law: 2008 Farm Bill (P.L. 110-246)	Current Law: 2014 Farm Bill (P.L. 113-79)
engaged if they receive income based on the farm's operating results, without providing labor or management. Spouses are considered actively engaged if the other spouse meets the qualification, allowing payment limits to be doubled. [7 U.S.C. 1308-1]	Specifically allows for different limits for varying types of farming operations, based on considerations of size, nature, and management requirements of different farming types, changes in the nature of active personal management due to advancements in farming practices, and the impact of this regulation on the long-term viability of farming operations. Regulations shall not apply to entities made solely of family members. Conferees intend for regional differences and a range of activities performed to be considered. Regulations are to be promulgated within six months of enactment, and may apply beginning with the 2015 crop year. [Sec. 1604]
Adjusted Gross Income (AGI) Limitation	
Prohibits farm commodity program benefits to an individual or entity if adjusted gross income exceeds certain thresholds. For this purpose, AGI is divided into two parts: farm AGI and non-farm AGI. Uses a 3-year average when comparing to the limit. —\$500,000 limit on non-farm AGI to qualify for and receive any farm commodity program benefits, Milk Income Loss Contract (MILC) program, noninsured crop assistance (NAP), or disaster payments. —\$750,000 limit on farm AGI to qualify for and receive direct payments, but counter-cyclical, ACRE and marketing loan benefits may continue if farm AGI exceeds \$750,000. [7 U.S.C. 1308-3a(b)(1)] For FY2012 only, a separate, additional \$1 million AGI limit applies to direct payments [P.L. 112-55, Sec. 745] For conservation programs, \$1 million limit on non-farm AGI, unless more than 66.66% of AGI is farm AGI. Provides USDA discretion to waive the limit for "environmentally sensitive land of special significance." [7 U.S.C. 1308-3a(b)(2)]	Eliminates the distinction between non-farm AGI and farm AGI, and establishes a limit on total AGI. Uses a 3-year average when comparing to the limit. Repeals expiration date of applicability. —\$900,000 limit on total AGI to qualify for and receive PLC or ARC payments, marketing loan gains or loan deficiency payments, supplemental agricultural disaster assistance, noninsured crop assistance, and (beginning in FY2015) conservation program payments. [Sec. 1605]
Supplemental Agricultural Disaster Assistance	
Beginning in 2008, five new disaster programs were authorized and funded for disasters occurring on or before 9/30/11. [7 U.S.C. 1531] Program funding derived from a transfer of 3.08% of annual customs receipts to the newly created Agricultural Disaster Relief Trust Fund. [19 U.S.C. 2497(a)] Under P.L. 112-240, all but SURE	All programs (except SURE) are reauthorized permanently (retroactive to FY2012) with mandatory funding from the Commodity Credit Corporation. Producers are not required to purchase crop insurance or NAP coverage. [Sec. 1501]

Prior Law: 2008 Farm Bill (P.L. 110-246)	Current Law: 2014 Farm Bill (P.L. 113-79)
(below) were reauthorized (but not funded) for FY2012 and FY2013. To be eligible, a producer must purchase crop insurance or coverage under the Noninsured Crop Disaster Assistance Program (NAP). No funding caps except for ELAP. The five programs:	
(1) Supplemental Revenue Assistance (SURE) Payments for crops (not just farm program crops); compensated producers for a portion of losses that are not eligible for an indemnity payment under a crop insurance policy; [7 U.S.C. 1531(b)]	No comparable provision.
(2) Livestock Indemnity Program (LIP) compensated ranchers at a rate of 75% of market value for livestock death losses in excess of the normal mortality due to adverse weather, including hurricanes, floods, blizzards, disease, wildfires, extreme heat, and extreme cold. [7 U.S.C. 1531(c)] Livestock includes: cattle (including dairy cattle), bison, poultry, sheep, swine, horses, and other livestock, as determined by the Secretary. [7 U.S.C. 1531(a)(12)]	Same a prior law except: (1) adds as an eligible loss attacks by animals reintroduced into the wild by the federal government or protected by federal law, including wolves and avian predators; and (2) ensures that LIP payments do not duplicate any federal compensation associated with federal quarantine and disposal. [Sec. 1501(b)]
(3) Livestock Forage Disaster Program (LFP) compensated eligible livestock producers for grazing losses due to either (a) qualifying drought conditions (using the drought monitor system for classifying drought), or (b) fire on public managed land. An eligible livestock producer is an owner, lessee, or contract grower that provides the pastureland or grazing land and meets other criteria. [7 U.S.C. 1531(d)] For drought, the monthly payment rate equals 60% of estimated feed costs; number of monthly payments: (a) 1 month for land located in a county with a D2 drought intensity for at least 8 consecutive weeks;	Same as prior law except as noted below. [Sec. 1501(c)]
(b) 2 months for land in a county with at least a D3 rating at any time during the normal grazing period;	Increased to 3 months of payments.
(c) 3 months if the county has a D3 rating for at least 4 weeks;	Increased to 4 months of payments.
(d) 3 months if the county has a D4 rating at any time during the normal grazing period.	Increased to 4 months of payments.
No comparable provision.	5 months of payments if the county has a D4 rating for at least 4 weeks.
Grazing losses must be on land that is native or improved pastureland, or is planted to a crop. Livestock in feedlots are not covered.	
For fire on public land, the monthly payment rate equaled to 50% of estimated feed costs and covered the period the federal agency excludes the producer from using the managed rangeland for grazing.	
(4) Emergency Assistance for Livestock, Honeybees, and Farm-Raised Catfish (ELAP) provided up to $50 million annually to compensate producers for disaster	Same as prior law except reduces maximum funding for ELAP to $20 million annually and adds cattle tick fever as a disease

Table A-1. (Continued)

Prior Law: 2008 Farm Bill (P.L. 110-246)	Current Law: 2014 Farm Bill (P.L. 113-79)
losses due to disease, adverse weather, or other conditions, such as blizzards, wildfires, and feed shortages not covered under SURE, LIP, or LFP. [7 U.S.C. 1531(e)]	covered by the program. [Sec. 1501(d)]
(5) Tree Assistance Program (TAP) provided payments to eligible orchardists and nursery growers who suffered tree mortality greater than 15% due to a natural disaster, including plant disease, insect infestation, drought, fire, freeze, flood, earthquake, lightning, or other occurrence. For damage or mortality in excess of 15%, reimbursement equals 70% of the cost of replanting trees (or sufficient seedlings to reestablish a stand) and 50% of the cost of pruning/removal to salvage existing trees or prepare the land to replant trees. [7 U.S.C. 1531(f)]	Same as prior law except TAP payment rate for replanting is reduced from 70% to 65%. [Sec. 1501(e)]
Disaster program payment limit: $100,000 per person per year for first four programs combined. [7 U.S.C. 1531(h)(2)] TAP has a separate limit of $100,000 per year, and TAP payment acreage may not exceed 500 acres. [7 U.S.C. 1531(f)(4)]	Combined payment limit is $125,000 per person for LIP, LFP, and ELAP. Separate limit of $125,000 applies to TAP, and 500 acre limit continues. [Sec. 1501(f)]
Adjusted gross income (AGI) limit: nonfarm AGI cannot exceed $500,000. [7 U.S.C. 1531(h)(3)] and [7 U.S.C. 1308-3a]	Adjusted gross income (AGI) limit: total AGI cannot exceed $900,000. [Sec. 1605(a)(2)]

Source: CRS.

Notes: Provisions for the dairy and sugar programs, as well as administrative provisions in Title I, are summarized in CRS Report R43076, The 2014 Farm Bill (P.L. 113- 79): Summary and Side-by-Side.

End Notes

[1] Separately, under the federal crop insurance program, covered commodities and more than 100 other crops, including fruits and vegetables, are also eligible for subsidized crop insurance, which provides within-year yield (or revenue) protection. That is, the guarantee is set each year just prior to planting the crop.

[2] For more background on the consequences of reverting to permanent law, see CRS Report R42442, Expiration and Extension of the 2008 Farm Bill.

[3] U.S. Department of Agriculture, Farm Service Agency, CCC Budget Essentials, FY2014 CCC Table 35, http://www.fsa.usda.gov/FSA/webapp?area=about&subject=landing&topic=bap-bu-cc.

[4] For background, see CRS Report R43336, Status of the WTO Brazil-U.S. Cotton Case.

[5] 7 C.F.R. 718.2.

[6] Base acre provisions since 1981 are described in Edwin Young et al., Economic Analysis of Base Acre and Payment Yield Designations Under the 2002 U.S. Farm Act, USDA

Economic Research Service, September 2005, pp. 36-41, http://www.ers.usda.gov /publications/err-economic-research-report/err12.aspx#.UzL3jYUq4Vc.

[7] Specifically, for each crop year, generic base acres are attributed to (i.e. temporarily designated as) base acres to a particular covered commodity base in proportion to that covered crop's share of total plantings of all covered commodities in that year. However, if the total number of acres planted to all covered commodities on the farm does not exceed the generic base acres on the farm, only the amount of acreage actually planted to a covered commodity is eligible for payment.

[8] The exception is payments associated with generic base acres, whereby current plantings can affect payment acreage.

[9] For example, a typical share rental arrangement in some regions is a two-thirds/one-third split of the crop harvested, with the landlord supplying all of the land and one-third of the cost of certain inputs such as fertilizer. The tenant supplies all of the labor and pays the remaining share of the input costs. Management decisions, such as crop diversification, are usually made jointly.

[10] C. Nickerson et al., "Trends in U.S. Farmland Values and Ownership," Economic Information Bulletin Number 92, USDA Economic Research Service, February 2012, http://www.ers.usda.gov/media/377487/eib92_2_.pdf.

[11] The exception is payments on "generic" base acres (formerly cotton base acres), which are directly attributable to the planted crop(s) until the total of the covered commodities planted on the farm exceed the generic base. If covered crop plantings are greater than the generic base, payment acres are attributed based on the proportion of the covered commodities planted.

[12] For a description of the calculations, see 2014 farm bill Section 1117(b)(2) and Section 1117(c)(3) in the Appendix. An example of ARC-individual coverage is available in Jonathan Coppess, "Farm Bill Programs in the 2014 Farm Bill," Farmdoc Webinar, March 5, 2014, http://www.farmdoc.illinois.edu/webinars.

[13] The market price is the adjusted world market price for upland cotton and rice, the national posted price for peanuts, national or regional posted prices for pulse crops, and the posted county price for most other commodities.

[14] Farmers may also forfeit the crop pledged as collateral to the government at the end of the loan period. This type of loan is called nonrecourse. A few crops are eligible only for recourse loans (i.e., must be repaid at principal plus interest), including ELS cotton, seed cotton, and high-moisture grains. Recourse loans are not eligible for a subsidy but do offer low-interest financing.

[15] See CRS Report R43336, Status of the WTO Brazil-U.S. Cotton Case.

[16] USDA Farm Service Agency, What's in the 2014 Farm Bill for Farm Service Agency Customers, Fact Sheet, Washington, DC, March 2014, http://www.fsa.usda.gov/Internet/FSA_File/2014_farm_bill_customers.pdf. Examples for universities and state extension service include http://www.farmdoc.illinois.edu/; http://www.farmdoc.illinois.edu/webinars/index.asp; and http://www.afpc.tamu.edu/.

[17] Tom Vilsack, "Secretary Vilsack Addresses Commodity Classic on Farm Bill Implementation," San Antonio, Texas, February 28, 2014, http://www.usda.gov/wps/portal/usda/usdahome?contentid=2014/02/0032.xml.

In: The Farm Safety Net: Key Components
Editor: Jodie R. Haggard
ISBN: 978-1-63463-731-2

Chapter 3

AGRICULTURAL DISASTER ASSISTANCE*

Dennis A. Shields

SUMMARY

The U.S. Department of Agriculture (USDA) offers several programs to help farmers recover financially from natural disasters, including drought and floods. All the programs have permanent authorization, and only one requires a federal disaster designation (the emergency loan program). Most programs receive funding amounts that are "such sums as necessary" and are not subject to annual discretionary appropriations.

The federal crop insurance program offers subsidized policies designed to protect crop producers from unavoidable risks associated with adverse weather, and weather-related plant diseases and insect infestations. Policies must be purchased prior to the planting season. Eligible commodities include most major crops and many specialty crops (including fruit, tree nut, vegetable, and nursery crops), as well as forage and pastureland for livestock producers. The enacted 2014 farm bill (the Agricultural Act of 2014; P.L. 113-79) enhances the crop insurance program by expanding its scope, covering a greater share of farm losses, and making other modifications that broaden policy coverage. Producers who grow a crop that is currently ineligible for crop insurance may apply for the Noninsured Crop Disaster Assistance Program (NAP).

---

* This is an edited, reformatted and augmented version of a Congressional Research Service publication RS21212, prepared for Members and Committees of Congress, dated August 27, 2014.

The 2014 farm bill also permanently authorizes three disaster programs for livestock and one for fruit trees, making nearly all parts of the U.S. farm sector covered by a standing disaster program. The programs cover losses beginning in FY2012. USDA began signup on April 15, 2014, ahead of other farm bill programs. Producers do not pay a fee to participate. The programs are:

1) the Livestock Indemnity Program (LIP), which provides payments to eligible livestock owners and contract growers at a rate of 75% of market value for livestock deaths in excess of normal mortality caused by adverse weather;
2) the Livestock Forage Disaster Program (LFP), which makes payments to eligible livestock producers who have suffered grazing losses on drought-affected pasture or grazing land, or on rangeland managed by a federal agency due to a qualifying fire;
3) the Emergency Assistance for Livestock, Honey Bees, and Farm-Raised Fish Program (ELAP), which provides payments (capped at $20 million per year) to producers of livestock, honey bees, and farm-raised fish as compensation for losses due to disease, adverse weather, and feed or water shortages; and
4) the Tree Assistance Program (TAP), making payments to orchardists/nursery tree growers for losses in excess of 15% to replant trees, bushes, and vines damaged by natural disasters.

Separately, for all types of farms and ranches, when a county has been declared a disaster area by either the President or the Secretary of Agriculture, producers in that county may become eligible for low-interest emergency disaster (EM) loans.

USDA has several permanent disaster assistance programs that help producers repair damaged land following natural disasters. It also has authority (prohibited in FY2014) to issue disaster payments to farmers with funds from "Section 32" or the Commodity Credit Corporation (CCC). Finally, USDA can use a variety of existing programs to address disaster issues as they arise, such as allowing emergency grazing on land enrolled in the Conservation Reserve Program.

The U.S. Department of Agriculture (USDA) has at its disposal several programs designed to help farmers and ranchers recover from the financial effects of natural disasters. These are (1) federal crop insurance, (2) the Noninsured Crop Disaster Assistance Program (NAP), (3) livestock and fruit tree disaster programs, and (4) emergency disaster loans for both crop and livestock producers. All have permanent authorization, and the emergency loan program is the only one requiring a federal disaster designation. Most programs receive funding amounts of "such sums as necessary" and are not subject to annual discretionary appropriations.

With enactment of the permanent livestock/fruit tree disaster programs in the 2014 farm bill (P.L. 113-79), nearly all segments of the U.S. farm sector are now covered by a standing disaster program. The array of federal programs, summarized in *Table 1*, reduces the potential need for emergency assistance that Congress previously provided to farmers and ranchers in the form of ad hoc disaster payments.[1]

FEDERAL CROP INSURANCE

The federal crop insurance program is administered by USDA's Risk Management Agency. The program is designed to protect crop producers from unavoidable risks associated with adverse weather, and weather-related plant diseases and insect infestations. Crop insurance is available for most major crops and many specialty crops (including fruit, tree nut, vegetable, and nursery crops), as well as forage and pastureland for livestock producers. A producer who chooses to purchase an insurance policy must do so by an administratively determined deadline date, which varies by crop and usually coincides with the planting season. Insurance products that protect against loss in revenue (yield times price) are also available. Policies are typically available in major growing regions.

The federal crop insurance program was instituted in the 1930s and was subject to major legislative reforms in 1980, and again in 1994 and 2000. The Agriculture Risk Protection Act of 2000 (P.L. 106-224) pumped $8.2 billion in new federal spending over a five-year period into the program primarily through more generous premium subsidies to help make the program more affordable to farmers and enhance farmer participation levels, in an effort to preclude the need for ad-hoc emergency disaster payments. Between 2006 and 2011, the federal cost of the crop insurance program averaged $5.9 billion per year, up from an annual average of $3.0 billion during 2000-2005. In 2012, high commodity prices drove up premiums subsidies and persistent drought resulted in large losses for the program. USDA estimated total program cost at $14.1 billion in FY2012. More favorable weather in 2013 reduced losses and reduced USDA's estimated total program costs to $6.0 billion in FY2013.

Table 1. USDA's Agricultural Disaster Assistance Programs (all programs permanently authorized—disaster designation required only for loans)

Program and Agency	Commodity Coverage and Requirements	Payment Trigger	Timing and Funding
Crop insurance indemnifies yield or revenue losses—RMA.	More than 100 crops are eligible; also covered are livestock margins & pasture. Producer must purchase a subsidized policy prior to planting.	Yield or revenue loss greater than the deductible (e.g., 30%) specified in the policy.	Indemnity payment issued after claim is filed, adjusted, and processed; unlimited funding.
Noninsured Crop Disaster Assistance Program (NAP) issues payments for yield loss—FSA.	Available for crops not currently eligible for crop ins. Producer pays fee prior to planting.	Yield loss in excess of 50%; additional coverage available.	Payment issued after claim is filed and processed; unlimited funding.
2014 farm bill programs issue payments for qualifying losses—FSA			
Livestock Indemnity Program (LIP); payments for livestock death losses	Beef and dairy cattle, hogs, chickens, ducks,. geese, turkeys, sheep, goats, alpacas, deer, elk, emus, and equine; no fee.	Livestock deaths in excess of normal mortality caused by adverse weather.	Payment issued after application is processed; unlimited funding.
Livestock Forage Disaster Program (LFP); payments for grazing losses from drought/fire.	Drought-affected pastureland and cropland planted for grazing; rangeland managed by a federal agency due to a qualifying fire; no fee.	Drought intensity level for an individual county, as published in the U.S. Drought Monitor.	Payment issued after application is processed; unlimited funding.
Emergency Assistance for Livestock, Honey Bees, and Farm-Raised Fish Program (ELAP); payments for losses not covered by LIP/LFP.	Livestock, honey bees, and farm-raised fish; losses may be caused by disease, adverse weather, feed or water shortages, or wildfires; no fee.	Bee losses in excess of normal mortality; certain losses for livestock, including feed and water costs.	Payment issued after application is processed; annual funding capped at $20 million.
Tree Assistance Program (TAP); payments	Trees, bushes, and vines from which an annualfor tree and vine losses. crop is produced; no fee.	Tree/vine mortality loss or damage in excess of 15%.	Payment issued after application is processed; unlimited funding.
Emergency (EM)	Damage to crops,	County disaster	Loan application due

Program and Agency	Commodity Coverage and Requirements	Payment Trigger	Timing and Funding
disaster loans offer low-interest	livestock, equipment or	declaration by	within 8 mo.
financing for production or physical losses—FSA.	farmland when commercial credit not available.	President, Secretary, or FSA; 30% crop loss or a physical loss.	of disaster; funding subject to annual appropriations.
Disaster Set-Aside (DSA) allows deferred loan	One full year's loan payment can be moved to	Disaster declaration by	Upon declaration of disaster.
payment for direct loans—FSA.	end of loan.	President, Secretary, or FSA.	

Source: CRS Report RS21212, Agricultural Disaster Assistance.

Notes: RMA = Risk Management Agency; FSA = Farm Service Agency. USDA also offers emergency land assistance: Emergency Conservation Program (ECP) and the Emergency Forest Restoration Program (EFRP), administered by FSA; Emergency Watershed Protection (EWP) program and EWP floodplain easement program, administered by the Natural Resources Conservation Service and the U.S. Forest Service. See CRS Report R42854, Emergency Assistance for Agricultural Land Rehabilitation.

Under the current crop insurance program, a producer who grows an insurable crop selects a level of crop yield and price coverage and pays a premium that increases as the levels of yield and price coverage rise. However, all eligible producers can receive catastrophic (CAT) coverage without paying a premium. The premium for this portion of coverage is completely subsidized by the federal government. Under CAT coverage, participating producers can receive a payment equal to 55% of the estimated market price of the commodity, on crop losses in excess of 50% of normal yield, or 50/55 coverage.

Although eligible producers do not have to pay a premium for CAT coverage, they are required to pay upon enrollment a $300 administrative fee per covered crop for each county where they grow the crop. The fee can be waived by USDA for financial hardship cases. Any producer who opts for CAT coverage has the opportunity to purchase additional insurance coverage from a private crop insurance company. For an additional premium paid by the producer, and partially subsidized by the government, a producer can increase the 50/55 catastrophic coverage to any equivalent level of coverage between

50/100 and 85/100 (i.e., 85% of yield and 100% of the estimated market price), in increments of 5%.

For many insurable commodities, an eligible producer can purchase revenue insurance. Under such a policy, a farmer potentially can receive an indemnity payment when actual farm revenue falls below the target level of revenue, regardless of whether the shortfall in revenue was caused by poor production or low farm commodity prices. Insured producers also can be eligible for reduced coverage if they are late or prevented from planting because of flooding.

The enacted 2014 farm bill (the Agricultural Act of 2014; P.L. 113-79) enhances the federal crop insurance program by expanding its scope, covering a greater share of farm losses, and making other modifications that broaden policy coverage. A prominent feature of the legislation is authorization of policies designed to reimburse "shallow losses"—an insured producer's out-of-pocket loss associated with the policy deductible. A new crop insurance policy called Stacked Income Protection Plan (STAX) is made available for upland cotton producers, while the Supplemental Coverage Option (SCO) is made available for other crops.

NONINSURED CROP DISASTER ASSISTANCE PROGRAM (NAP)

Producers who grow a crop that is currently ineligible for crop insurance may apply for the Noninsured Crop Disaster Assistance Program (NAP). NAP has permanent authority under Section 196 of the Federal Agriculture Improvement and Reform Act of 1996 (7 U.S.C. 7333), and is administered by USDA's Farm Service Agency. It was first authorized under the Federal Crop Insurance Reform Act of 1994 (P.L. 103-354). NAP is not subject to annual appropriations. Instead, it receives such sums as are necessary through USDA's Commodity Credit Corporation, which has a line of credit with the U.S. Treasury to fund an array of farm programs.

Eligible crops under NAP include any commercial crops grown for food, fiber, or livestock consumption that are ineligible for crop insurance, and include mushrooms, floriculture, ornamental nursery, Christmas tree crops, turfgrass sod, aquaculture, and ginseng. Trees grown for wood paper or pulp products are not eligible. To be eligible for a NAP payment, a producer first must apply for coverage by the application closing date, which varies by crop, but is generally about 30 days prior to the final planting date for an annual crop. Like catastrophic crop insurance, NAP applicants must also pay an administrative fee. The NAP fee is $250 per crop payable at the time of application.[2]

In order to receive a NAP payment, a producer must experience at least a 50% crop loss caused by a natural disaster, or be prevented from planting more than 35% of intended crop acreage. For any losses in excess of the minimum loss threshold, a producer can receive 55% of the average market price for the covered commodity. Hence, NAP is similar to catastrophic crop insurance coverage in that it pays 55% of the market price for losses in excess of 50% of normal historic production.

In order to expand coverage for specialty crops and others covered under NAP, the 2014 farm bill provides additional coverage at 50% to 65% of established yield and 100% of average market price. The farmer-paid fee for additional coverage is 5.25% times the product of the selected coverage level and value of production (acreage times yield times average market price).

A producer of a noninsured crop is subject to a payment limit of $125,000 per person under NAP and is ineligible for a payment if the producer's total adjusted gross income exceeds $900,000. The total federal cost of NAP was $234 million in FY2012 and $342 million in FY2013, and is estimated at $154 million for FY2014.[3]

2014 Farm Bill Disaster Programs

Section 1501 of the 2014 farm bill (P.L. 113-79) permanently authorizes four agricultural disaster programs for livestock and fruit trees. They are (1) the Livestock Indemnity Program (LIP); (2) the Livestock Forage Disaster Program (LFP); (3) the Emergency Assistance for Livestock, Honey Bees, and Farm-Raised Fish Program (ELAP); and (4) the Tree Assistance Program (TAP). The programs, originally established in the 2008 farm bill for only four years, have been authorized retroactively (with no expiration date) to cover losses beginning in FY2012.[4] They operate nationwide and are administered by USDA's Farm Service Agency.

All programs except ELAP receive uncapped mandatory funding via the Commodity Credit Corporation. That is, LIP, LFP, and TAP receive "such sums as necessary" to reimburse eligible producers for their losses. ELAP is capped at $20 million per year. For losses in FY2012- FY2014, payments through August 1, 2014, have totaled $1.8 billion for LFP and $39 million for LIP.

Livestock producers traditionally have not been covered by crop insurance or other forms of federal support, and the farm bill disaster programs have been designed to reimburse them for some of their financial losses due to weather events (and disease in the case of ELAP). Producers do not pay a fee to participate.

For individual producers, combined payments under all programs (except TAP) may not exceed $125,000 per year. For TAP, a separate limit of $125,000 per year applies. Also, to be eligible for a payment, a producer's total adjusted gross income cannot exceed $900,000.

USDA issued its final rule for all four programs on April 14, 2014.[5] Program signup began April 15, 2014. Producers can apply at their local Farm Service Agency office.[6]

Average annual federal payments under the 2008 farm bill were $38 million for LIP, $142 million per year for LFP, $10 million for ELAP, and $5 million for TAP.

Livestock Indemnity Program (LIP)

The Livestock Indemnity Program (LIP) provides payments to eligible livestock owners and contract growers for livestock deaths in excess of normal mortality caused by adverse weather. The 2014 farm bill added a provision to cover attacks by animals reintroduced into the wild by the federal government or protected by federal law.

Eligible livestock include beef and dairy cattle, hogs, chickens, ducks, geese, turkeys, sheep, goats, alpacas, deer, elk, emus, and equine. The livestock must have been maintained for commercial use and not produced for reasons other than commercial use as part of a farming operation. The program excludes wild free-roaming animals, pets, and animals used for recreational purposes, such as hunting, roping, or for show.

The LIP payment rate is equal to 75% of the market value of the animal. USDA publishes a payment rate for each type of livestock for each year (e.g., $1,223.45 per beef cow and $4.12 per duck in 2014).[7] For eligible livestock contract growers, the payment rate is based on 75% of the average income loss sustained by the contract grower, less any monetary compensation received from the contractor for the loss of income.

Livestock Forage Disaster Program (LFP)

The Livestock Forage Disaster Program (LFP) makes payments to eligible livestock producers who have suffered grazing losses on drought-affected pastureland (including cropland planted specifically for grazing), or on rangeland managed by a federal agency due to a qualifying fire.

Eligible producers must own, cash or share lease, or be a contract grower of covered livestock during the 60 calendar days before the beginning date of a qualifying drought or fire. They must also provide pastureland or grazing land for covered livestock that is either (a) physically located in a county affected by a qualifying drought during the normal grazing period for the county, or (b) managed by a federal agency where grazing is not permitted due to fire.

Eligible livestock types are livestock that have been (or would have been) grazing on eligible grazing land or pastureland. These include alpacas, beef cattle, buffalo, beefalo, dairy cattle, sheep, deer, elk, emus, equine, goats, llamas, poultry, reindeer, and swine. The livestock must have been maintained for commercial use as part of a farming operation; and livestock owned for noncommercial uses are excluded. Also, livestock that were (or would have been) in a feedlot are not eligible.

Payments are generally triggered by the drought intensity level for an individual county, as published in the U.S. Drought Monitor, a federal report published each week. The number of monthly payments depends on the drought severity and length of time the county has been designated as such (*Table 2*). For drought, the payment amount is equal to the number of monthly payments *times* 60% of estimated monthly feed cost. For producers who sold livestock because of drought conditions, the payment rate is equal to 80% of the estimated monthly feed cost.[8]

Emergency Assistance for Livestock, Honey Bees, and Farm-Raised Fish Program (ELAP)

The Emergency Assistance for Livestock, Honey Bees, and Farm-Raised Fish Program (ELAP) provides payments to producers of livestock, honey bees, and farm-raised fish as compensation for losses due to disease, adverse weather, feed or water shortages, or other conditions, such as wildfires, that are not covered under the Livestock Indemnity Program (LIP) or the Livestock Forage Program (LFP).[9] The 2014 farm bill added a provision to cover cattle tick fever. Total funding for ELAP is capped at $20 million per year.

Table 2. Livestock Forage Program (LFP)

Drought Monitor Intensity	Time Period	No. of Monthly Payments
D2 (severe drought)	For at least eight consecutive weeks during the normal grazing period	one monthly payment
D3 (extreme drought)	At any time during the normal grazing period	three monthly payments
D3 (extreme drought)	For at least four weeks during the normal grazing period	four monthly payments
D4 (exceptional drought)	At any time during the normal grazing period	four monthly payments
D4 (exceptional drought)	For four weeks (not necessarily consecutive) during the normal grazing period	five monthly payments

Source: P.L. 113-79, Section 1501(e).

Notes: Drought intensity level can apply to any area of a county. The LFP monthly payment rate for drought is equal to 60% of the lesser of the monthly feed cost based on either (a) corn prices, specified feeding requirements, and number of animals; or (b) the normal carrying capacity of the land. For details on monthly feed costs and examples, see FSA handbook at http://www.fsa.usda.gov/Internet/FSA_File/1-ldap_r01_a01.pdf. In the case of a producer who sold livestock because of drought conditions, the payment rate is equal to 80% of the monthly feed cost. For fire on federally managed rangeland, the payment rate is 50% of the monthly feed cost, adjusted for the number of days the producer is prohibited from grazing (not to exceed 180 days).

ELAP specifically provides assistance for the loss of honey bee colonies in excess of normal mortality. In order to meet the eligibility requirements for honey bee colony losses, they must be the direct result of an eligible adverse weather or loss condition such as colony collapse disorder (CCD), eligible winter storm, excessive wind, and flood. For livestock losses, four categories are covered by ELAP: (1) livestock death losses caused by an eligible loss condition, (2) livestock feed and grazing losses that are not due to drought or wildfires on federally managed lands, (3) losses resulting from the additional cost of transporting water to livestock due to an eligible drought, and (4) losses resulting from the additional cost associated with gathering livestock for treatment related to cattle tick fever.

Tree Assistance Program (TAP)

The Tree Assistance Program (TAP) makes payments to qualifying orchardists and nursery tree growers to replant or rehabilitate trees, bushes, and vines damaged by natural disasters. Eligible trees, bushes, and vines are those from which an annual crop is produced for commercial purposes. Nursery trees include ornamental, fruit, nut, and Christmas trees produced for commercial sale. Trees used for pulp or timber are ineligible.

To be considered an eligible loss, the individual stand must have sustained a mortality loss or damage loss in excess of 15% after adjustment for normal mortality or damage, to be determined based on (a) each eligible disaster event, except for losses due to plant disease; or (b) for plant disease, the time period for which the stand is infected. Also, the loss could not have been prevented through reasonable and available measures.

For tree, bush, or vine replacement, replanting and/or rehabilitation, the payment calculation is the lesser of (a) 65% of the actual cost of replanting (in excess of 15% mortality) and/or 50% of the actual cost of rehabilitation (in excess of 15% damage), or (b) the maximum eligible amount established for the practice by the Farm Service Agency. The total quantity of acres planted to trees, bushes, or vines for which a producer can receive TAP payments cannot exceed 500 acres annually.[10]

EMERGENCY DISASTER LOANS

When a county has been declared a disaster area by either the President or the Secretary of Agriculture, agricultural producers in that county may become eligible for low-interest emergency disaster (EM) loans available through USDA's Farm Service Agency (FSA).[11] Producers in counties that are contiguous to a county with a disaster designation also become eligible for an EM loan. EM loan funds may be used to help eligible farmers, ranchers, and aquaculture producers recover from *production* losses (when the producer suffers a significant loss of an annual crop) or from *physical* losses (such as repairing or replacing damaged or destroyed structures or equipment, or for the replanting of permanent crops such as orchards). A qualified applicant can then borrow up to 100% of actual production or physical losses (not to exceed $500,000) at an interest rate of 2.25%.

Once a county is declared eligible, an individual producer within the county (or a contiguous county) must also meet the following requirements for an EM loan. A producer must (1) be a family farmer and a citizen or permanent resident of the United States; (2) experience a crop loss of more than 30% or a physical loss of livestock, livestock products, real estate, or property; and (3) be unable to obtain credit from a commercial lender, but still show the potential to repay the loan. Applications must be received within eight months of the county's disaster designation date. Loans for non-real estate purposes generally must be repaid within 1 to 7 years; loans for physical losses to real estate have terms up to 20 years. Depending on the repayment ability of the producer and other circumstances, these terms can be extended to 20 years for non-real estate losses and up to 40 years for real estate losses.

The EM loan program is permanently authorized by Title III of the Consolidated Farm and Rural Development Act (P.L. 87-128), as amended, and is subject to annual appropriations. In the FY2014 Consolidated Appropriations Act (P.L. 113-76), emergency loan authority was provided at $35 million, an increase of $13 million from FY2013, which was the first year in many years that emergency loans received new loan authority. Emergency loans had been operating for much of the last decade, through FY2012, on unused EM funds carried over from previous fiscal years. Total EM loans (made) are typically less than $100 million per year.

Also in counties with disaster designations, producers who have existing direct loans with FSA may be eligible for Disaster Set-Aside (DSA). If, as a result of disaster, a customer is unable to pay all expenses and make loan payments that are coming due, up to one full year's payment can be moved to the end of the loan.[12]

OTHER USDA ASSISTANCE

In addition to farm assistance described in previous sections, USDA also has several permanent disaster assistance programs that help producers repair damaged land following natural disasters. It also has authority to issue disaster payments to farmers with "Section 32" or "CCC" funds and can use a variety of existing programs to address disaster issues as they arise.

Emergency Agricultural Land Assistance Programs

Several USDA programs offer financial and technical assistance to producers to repair, restore, and mitigate damage by a natural disaster on private land.

- The Emergency Conservation Program (ECP) and the Emergency Forest Restoration Program (EFRP) are administered by USDA's Farm Service Agency. For both programs, participants are paid a percentage of the cost to restore the land to a productive state. ECP also funds water for livestock and installing water conserving measures during times of drought. EFRP was created to assist private forestland owners with losses caused by a natural disaster on nonindustrial private forest land.
- The Emergency Watershed Protection (EWP) program and the EWP floodplain easement program are administered by USDA's Natural Resources Conservation Service and the U.S. Forest Service. EWP assists sponsors, landowners, and operators in implementing emergency recovery measures for runoff retardation and erosion prevention to relieve imminent hazards to life and property created by a natural disaster. The EWP floodplain easement program is a mitigation program that pays for permanent easements on private land meant to safeguard lives and property from future floods, drought, and the products of erosion.

"Section 32" and "CCC" Funds for Farm Disaster Payments

USDA has authority to distribute emergency payments to farmers with "Section 32" and Commodity Credit Corporation (CCC) funds. However, in annual appropriations acts since FY2012 (most recently, Section 719 of FY2014 Agriculture appropriations, P.L. 113-76), Congress has prohibited the use of appropriated funds to pay for salaries and expenses needed to operate a farm disaster program under either of these two funding sources.[13]

- USDA's "Section 32" program is funded by a permanent appropriation of 30% of the previous year's customs receipts, and funds are used for a variety of activities, including child nutrition programs, the purchase of commodities for domestic food programs, and farm disaster relief. The statutory authority is Section 32 of the Agricultural Adjustment Act Amendment of 1935 (P.L.74-320, 7 U.S.C. 612c). The authority to provide disaster relief is attributed to Clause 3 of Section 32, which provides that funds "shall be used to re-establish farmers' purchasing power by making payments in connections with the normal production." Section 32 was most recently used for disaster payments when USDA made payments of $348 million for 2009 crop losses for rice, upland cotton, soybeans, and sweet potatoes.[14]

- The Commodity Credit Corporation (CCC) is the funding mechanism for the mandatory subsidy payments that farmers receive. It was federally chartered by the CCC Charter Act of 1948 (P.L.80-806). The authority to provide disaster relief is attributed to Section 5 of the act (15 U.S.C. 714c), which authorizes the CCC to support the prices of agricultural commodities through loans, purchases, payments, and other operations.

Examples of Adjustments to Existing USDA Programs

USDA can use authority under existing programs to help producers recover from natural disasters. For example, in response to the major drought affecting a large part of the United States in 2012, USDA took a number of actions, including[15]

- extended emergency grazing on Conservation Reserve Program (CRP) acres;[16]
- reduced the emergency loan interest rate and made emergency loans available earlier in the season;
- allowed haying or grazing of cover crops without any penalty on the insurability of planted 2013 spring crops;
- worked with crop insurance companies to provide flexibility to farmers; and
- transferred $14 million in unobligated program funds into the Emergency Conservation Program to help farmers and ranchers rehabilitate farmland damaged by natural disasters and for carrying out emergency water conservation measures in periods of severe drought.

More recently, in addition to implementing the 2014 farm bill disaster programs, USDA has taken a number of administrative actions in 2014 to assist producers in California and elsewhere dealing with drought.[17] These include

- $15 million in targeted conservation assistance through the Environmental Quality Incentives Program (EQIP) for the most extreme and exceptional drought areas; funding helps farmers and ranchers implement conservation practices that conserve water resources, reduce wind erosion on drought-impacted fields and improve livestock access to water;
- $5 million in targeted Emergency Watershed Protection (EWP) Program assistance to the most drought impacted areas of California to protect vulnerable soils; and
- $3 million in Emergency Water Assistance Grants for rural communities experiencing water shortages.[18]

End Notes

[1] Ad hoc assistance was made available primarily through emergency supplemental appropriations to a wide array of USDA programs. For a history of the congressional response to agricultural disasters, see CRS Report RL31095, Emergency Funding for Agriculture: A Brief History of Supplemental Appropriations, FY1989-FY2012.

[2] For more on NAP, see the USDA factsheet at http://www.fsa.usda.gov/Internet/ FSA_File/ nap_august_2011.pdf.

[3] U.S. Department of Agriculture, http://www.obpa.usda.gov/26ccc2015notes.pdf.

[4] A comparison of the disaster program provisions of the 2008 and 2014 farm bills is in CRS Report R43448, Farm Commodity Provisions in the 2014 Farm Bill (P.L. 113-79), by Dennis A. Shields. The largest of the farm disaster assistance programs authorized by the 2008 farm bill was the Supplemental Revenue Assistance Payments Program (SURE). The program was designed to compensate eligible producers for a portion of crop losses that are not eligible for an indemnity payment under the crop insurance program (i.e., the portion of losses that is part of the deductible on the policy). Given the complexity of the program and concerns about its effectiveness, the SURE program was not reauthorized in the 2014 farm bill. However, elements of it were included in the Agriculture Risk Coverage (ARC) program for "covered crops" (i.e., farm program crops) by offering producers a farm-level revenue guarantee on the combined crop revenue on each farm.

[5] Commodity Credit Corporation, U.S. Department of Agriculture, "Supplemental Agricultural Disaster Assistance Programs, Payment Limitations, and Payment Eligibility," 79 Federal Register 21086-21118, April 14, 2014.

[6] For local Farm Service Agency contact information, see http://offices.sc.egov.usda.gov/locator/ app?agency=fsa.

[7] Payment rates are available in the USDA fact sheet at http://www.fsa.usda.gov/ Internet/FSA_File/ lip_long_fact_sht_2014.pdf. For more information, see 7 C.F.R. §1416 Subpart D—Livestock Indemnity Program; and Also, program details and producer examples for all livestock disaster programs are in the USDA/FSA handbook, http://www. fsa.usda.gov/Internet/FSA_File/1-ldap_r01_a01.pdf.

[8] For more information on LFP, see 7 C.F.R. §1416 Subpart C—Livestock Forage Disaster Program; and the USDA fact sheet at https://www.fsa.usda. gov/Internet/ FSA_ File/lfp_long_fact_sht_2014.pdf.

[9] For more information on ELAP, see 7 C.F.R. §1416 Subpart B—Emergency Assistance for Livestock, Honeybees, and Farm-Raised Fish Program; USDA fact sheet for honey bees at http://www.fsa.usda.gov/Internet/FSA_File/ elap_honeybee_fact_sht.pdf; USDA fact sheet for livestock assistance at http://www.fsa.usda.gov/Internet/FSA_File/ elap_livestk_ fact_sht.pdf and USDA fact sheet for farm-raised fish assistance at http://www.fsa. usda.gov/Internet/ FSA_File/elap_livestk_fish.pdf.

[10] For more information on TAP, see 7 C.F.R. §1416 Subpart E—Tree Assistance Program; and the USDA fact sheet at http://www.fsa.usda.gov/Internet/FSA_File/tap_2014.pdf. Also, program details and producer examples are in the USDA/FSA handbook, http://www. fsa.usda.gov/Internet/FSA_File/1-tap_r04_a01.pdf.

[11] For an overview of the USDA emergency disaster designation and declaration process, see https://www.fsa.usda.gov/ Internet/FSA_File/ed_desig_process2012.pdf. For the USDA factsheet on EM loans, see https://www.fsa.usda.gov/ Internet/FSA_File/ emloanpr_ sept12.pdf.

[12] For more information, see USDA factsheet at http://www.fsa.usda.gov/ Internet/FSA_ File/debt_set_aside11.pdf.

[13] Congress can stop typically for a year at a time—via appropriations acts and without changing the underlying authorizations law—the ability of the executive branch to carry out a law by prohibiting the payments of salaries to implement a certain government function. See CRS Report R43110, Agriculture and Related Agencies: FY2014 and FY2013 (Post-Sequestration) Appropriations, coordinated by Jim Monke.

[14] USDA, Farm Service Agency, Crop Assistance Program (CAP) Fact Sheet, October 2010, http://www.fsa.usda.gov/ Internet/FSA_File/cap10pfs.pdf.

[15] USDA, Farm Service Agency, "USDA Designates Del Norte County in California as a Primary Natural Disaster Area With Assistance to Producers in Oregon," press release, February 5, 2014, http://www.fsa.usda.gov/FSA/ newsReleases?area=newsroom&subject =landing&topic=edn&newstype=ednewsrel&type=detail&item= ed_20140205_rel_0020.html.

[16] CRS Report R42783, Conservation Reserve Program (CRP): Status and Issues, by Megan Stubbs.

[17] U.S. Department of Agriculture, "Obama Administration Announces Additional Assistance to Californians Impacted by Drought," press release, February 14, 2014, http://www.usda.gov /wps/portal/usda/usdahome?contentidonly=true& contentid=2014/02/0022.xml.

[18] The U.S. Department of Agriculture's Rural Utilities Service (RUS) provides grants and loans for rural water systems in communities with less than 10,000 inhabitants; its programs are for domestic water service, not water for agricultural purposes. For more information, see CRS Report R43408, Emergency Water Assistance During Drought: Federal Non-Agricultural Programs, by Nicole T. Carter, Tadlock Cowan, and Joanna Barrett.

INDEX

#

A

B

C

D

E

F

G

H

I

L

M

N

S

T